how to
really LOVE
your
ADULT child

Jean Hewes

Gary Chapman, PhD & Ross Campbell, MD

Harold L Mast
12622 S. 700 E.
Converse, IN 46919

December 2016

how to
really LOVE
your
ADULT child

BUILDING A HEALTHY RELATIONSHIP

IN A CHANGING WORLD

NORTHFIELD PUBLISHING
CHICAGO

All Scripture quotations, unless indicated, are taken from the *Holy Bible: New International Version*®. NIV®. Copyright © 1973, 1978, 1984 by Biblica, Inc. Used by permission of Zondervan. All rights reserved worldwide.

Scripture quotations marked NASB are taken from the *New American Standard Bible,* © 1960, 1962, 1963, 1968, 1971, 1972, 1973, 1975, 1977, and 1995 by The Lockman Foundation. Used by permission. (www.Lockman.org)

2011 edition edited by Elizabeth Cody Newenhuyse
Cover and interior design: Smartt Guys design
Cover image: Stephen W. Morris / iStock
Gary Chapman photo: Alysia Grimes Photography/Ross Campbell photo: Boyce Shore & Associates

Library of Congress Cataloging-in-Publication Data
Campbell, Ross, 1936-
  How to really love your adult child : building a healthy relationship in a
changing world / Ross Campbell & Gary Chapman.
      p. cm.
  Rev. ed. of: Parenting your adult child : how you can help them achieve
their full potential. c1999.
  Includes bibliographical references and index.
  ISBN 978-0-8024-6851-2 (alk. paper)
  1. Parent and adult child. 2. Adult children–Family relationships. 3.
Parenting. 4. Parenting–Religious aspects–Christianity. I. Chapman, Gary
D., 1938- II. Campbell, Ross, 1936- Parenting your adult child. III. Title.
  HQ755.86.C353 2011
  306.874084'4–dc22
                    2010048994

Moody Publishers is committed to caring wisely for God's creation and uses recycled paper whenever possible. The paper in this book consists of 30 percent post-consumer waste.

We hope you enjoy this book from Northfield Publishing. Our goal is to provide high-quality, thought-provoking books and products that connect truth to your real needs and challenges. For more information on other books and products written and produced from a biblical perspective, go to www.moodypublishers.com or write to:

Northfield Publishing
820 N. LaSalle Boulevard
Chicago, IL 60610

1 3 5 7 9 10 8 6 4 2

Printed in the United States of America

To my wonderful children,
Carey, David, and Dale.
You have been my best teachers
during your growth to adulthood,
and you have shown me the wonder of parenthood.

To Shelley and Derek,
my children,
my friends!

contents

Introduction: Great Joy . . . or Great Pain   9

1. Getting to Know Today's Adult Child   15

2. When Your Adult Child Is Not Succeeding   25

3. When the Nest Isn't Emptying   39

4. When Your Child Moves Home   57

5. Major Hurdles to Independence   73

6. Conflicts over Lifestyle Issues   95

7. Becoming an In-law and a Grandparent   113

8. Meeting Your Own Needs   129

9. Building a Confident, Growing Relationship   147

10. Leaving Your Child a Positive Legacy   167

Notes   187

great JOY. . .
or great PAIN

When many of us were growing up, it was simply assumed that young people would "go forth to make their fortune in the world." Many, if not most, in the Builder and Boomer generations had a deep desire to do just that. The world was our oyster, calling us and welcoming us to find new frontiers and "make our mark." We sallied forth with eagerness, confident that we knew what was expected of us and that we could meet those expectations.

Things are different now. Life is less orderly, change is rampant, and the future more difficult to anticipate. We no longer live in a society of shared values, and ideological conflict is increasing. Our basic institutions that once provided stability are under attack and struggling to survive. Young people are very aware of the instability, and many of them feel anxious and pessimistic and want to extend the transition to adulthood and independence. And we as parents of adult children wonder, at times, what to do.

If you're a parent of an adult child, perhaps you're experiencing some of those shocks, adjustments, and, at times, pleasures of relating to your adult children. Gary remembers the first time he became aware of how adult children can bring their parents great joy or tremendous pain. He had left the airport in Charlotte, heading home on Interstate 85, when he decided to surprise his daughter at Davidson College, just off exit 123.

"I knew that she might not be in her dorm room, but it seemed a shame to be so close and not at least try. As I climbed the stairs to her third floor dormitory room, my heart was racing, not so much from the climb as from anticipation of surprising Shelley. *If she is not in,* I reasoned, *I can at least leave a note on the door and she would know that I was thinking about her.*"

Gary found his efforts rewarded when he knocked on the door. "She opened the door and said, 'Dad!' She and her friend Lisa were studying for an exam. I hugged them both, chatted for fifteen minutes, hugged them both again, slipped Shelley a twenty-dollar bill, and made my exit.

"Only fifteen minutes, but that brief encounter filled my mind with memories and emotions over the next hour as I resumed my drive home. I remembered her as a baby, always smiling—well, almost always. I visualized her as a three-year-old riding her tricycle in the Texas sun while I was in graduate school. I remembered kindergarten, first grade, and her eagerness to learn. I remembered all those years, including the day she was ten and announced to the family that when she grew up she was going to be a doctor and help people. . . . Now at twenty, there she was in college, enrolled in Davidson's premedical major, pursuing her dream. I confess that I could not hold back the tears of joy."

After dinner, Gary's wife, Karolyn, joined him at a family enrichment group at their church. A few parents talked about their experiences and present situations. One father's words to the group remain vivid:

"Our twenty-three-year-old son, Shawn, is in prison for selling drugs. We visited with him this afternoon and our hearts are heavy. On the one hand, we tend to blame ourselves. I do especially because I was so busy when he was growing up; I feel that I didn't spend enough time with him. On the other hand, we know that the choices he made were his own; but whoever bears the blame, the bottom line is it hurts to see him in prison."

As we write this book, we are aware that your adult children can bring tremendous joy or terrible pain. We write this book for you: parents of adult children and soon-to-be parents of young adult children. For more than thirty years, each of us has invested our professional lives in helping individuals and families cope with the stresses of contemporary life—Ross as a psychiatrist specializing in child and family practice, and Gary as a marriage and family counselor, and as a minister. We write from our involvement with hundreds of families over the years and also from experience with our own families. Along with our wives, we have raised our own children to adulthood: Ross has two married sons and one married daughter; Gary has a son and daughter, both married.

We are aware that there are thousands of Shelleys and Shawns; some have followed their dreams, and some have lost their way. As parents and counselors, we have seen parents facing increasing problems in preparing their children for adulthood. Later, as parents of adult children, they face additional challenges with their grown sons and daughters. To those parents, we desire to offer words of comfort and challenge.

This book is concerned with understanding the events of today—and yesteryear—that made this wonderful generation what they have become. We also will look at how parents can adjust and respond to adult children at home, such as the adult child who lives at home during college or while starting a job (or stays home for some other reason) and those children who return home years later.

Some of our adult children's choices can create tension, especially when they involve deep personal values, such as sexuality or religious beliefs. Such tensions can result in strong disagreement, even estrangement. Our responses can make a difference in their lives and in our relationships with them. (See chapter 6 for a discussion of how to respond to having your deeply held values challenged or even rejected.)

We also will explore how relationships change with our adult children when we become in-laws, and later, grandparents. How do we give advice—should we? Most grandparents are caught in a dilemma of helping two generations without being judgmental or overly intrusive. And some grandparents are even raising their own grandchildren. We will examine this phenomenon also.

The authors are writing from a Judeo-Christian worldview. Thus, where appropriate, we draw from the wisdom of the Hebrew and Greek Old and New Testaments. Both authors hold a Christian belief, but we welcome readers of all faiths to join us in exploring these critical areas. We hope that parents of all religious views will find in this work practical help in relating to their young adult children. Whatever our religious or cultural backgrounds, as parents we face many common struggles in seeking to relate positively to our adult children while at the same time maintaining our own mental and spiritual health.

Drawing from our counseling practices, family research, and our own experiences as parents, we seek to make this a practical handbook for parents concerned with developing positive, growing relationships with their young adult children.

As parents, we do not have the choice of being unconcerned. Someone has said, "The choice to be a parent is the choice to have your heart walking around outside your body as long as you live." You are concerned because they are a part of you. The question is, "How do I channel my concern?" That is the focus of this book.

getting to KNOW today's adult CHILD

Do you remember 1961? JFK brought a youthful style to the White House; the first astronauts went into space, and we all watched on black-and-white TV. Most agree life was simpler then; certainly our culture was far more predictable. Everyone knew the script—young people finished high school and either went to college or got a job. For some, their first job was in the military. With or without college, readily available full-time employment meant that independence was just around the corner. They would find their own apartment and start to save for the day when they married and began a family.

That was fifty years ago. Then, if you had an adult son or daughter, the grown child typically lived near you. After the child married (most married young), the young couple often would join the whole clan for Sunday dinner and for holidays at your home, though otherwise the young couple would live their own lives. As parents, now and then you might have watched the grandchildren, and when you retired, the grown children made their pilgrimage to Florida or California to see you, usually with grandkids in tow. Everyone knew their role and played it quite well. If life was not always happy, at least it was stable.

THOSE AMAZING MILLENNIALS

Fifty years ago, this book could not have been written. But things have changed during the past five decades, and the predictable is no more. It began with the tumultuous sixties that overturned a way of life Americans had taken for granted. The birth-control pill came first, followed by legal abortion; together they fueled the so-called sexual revolution. Vietnam and political intrigue led to Watergate and a disillusioned public. Divorce became commonplace, and the "traditional" family diminished in importance as our culture became more mobile and diverse.

Nowhere have these changes been more poignantly felt than by parents of those amazing and puzzling young people we call Generation Y (or the Millennials or the Mosaics), as well as some of the younger Gen Xers. Among the changes affecting the contour of the family circle are:

1. Adult children may live more than one hundred miles away, often out of state.
2. Or, adult children, increasingly, may be moving back to the nest— sometimes with their own children.
3. Many adult children don't marry until their late twenties or their thirties.
4. Some adult children have live-in partners of the opposite sex, sharing their lives and sometimes their checking accounts, but not marrying. They're convinced marriage is too risky, at least for a while.
5. Adult children may seem less driven than their parents.

It is easy enough to try to lay blame for the changing, unsettled times solely on uncontrollable factors. Yet many of today's boomer parents have to look no further than their own experiences in the sixties and seventies, and often the actions of their own parents. For it was then that some of their parents no longer felt compelled to stay in marriages that were not bringing them the emotional satisfaction they desired. Many young people decided that sex was too beautiful to be kept for marriage, that multiple partners were the wave of the future. The pleasures of recreational drug use and sexual experimentation drew many, and social stigmas waned.

Today 40 percent of our young adults grew up as children of divorce. The Gen Xers, in particular, were labeled latchkey children, because they had keys to their homes after school, as their parents were away, working. Many of these children were more often shuffled and managed than parented. The Millennial generation, as we will see, were the "baby on board," pampered generation, but their coming of age and seeming delaying of adulthood has also baffled parents.

With all these changes, many parents wonder now how to relate to their adult children. What is our role now? There are roles that parents can and should play in the lives of their adult children, as we plan to show in this book; but to play those roles, we need to better understand our grown sons and daughters. Let's begin by looking at the prevailing attitudes of our adult children.

THE GOOD LIFE?

Many of our young people want to establish a lifestyle similar to what their parents have, but they also see that, increasingly, the prospects for doing that are bleak, at least in the current economic crunch. We are all aware of the dismal unemployment statistics—by some measurements, young adults have suffered the most. Most of the jobs available are in the service categories, which do not offer a good wage. This means that great numbers of well-trained young people are looking for fewer and fewer high-paying positions.

Today's young adults may have watched their fathers or mothers loyally work for one or two employers in their careers. That is hardly an option anymore, and company loyalty to employees is pretty much a thing of the past. One factor in this is technology, which has led to downsizing, outsourcing, and greater competition in the marketplace. Another is the simple fact that many companies have found they can be more profitable with fewer employees.

Today's young people have a different idea of what constitutes "the good life." They want to travel and enjoy hobbies and sports. They want satisfying relationships and freedom to explore and do new things. They don't have much patience with the notion of working decades to gradually rise to the lifestyle their parents enjoy.

This may be one of the most confusing questions in society and also in our families. Many adult children saw their parents spend way too much time on work. And then they saw their parents, just when life should be in the reward stage, laid off, downsized, fired, or facing an uncertain retirement. And so both generations struggle and question.

STRUGGLING TO GROW UP?

Many adult children display a dependence on their parents that is foreign to an older generation. Indeed, some researchers even suggest that "emerging adulthood"—the life stage from about 18 to 30—is a separate developmental stage similar to adolescence, which was first identified early in the twentieth century. Certainly today's economy is one factor; however, this phenomenon has been growing for two decades. Whatever the reason, many young adults seem to be struggling to grow up. In asking for parental help, they seem to be saying, "I need more from you, Mom and Dad."

In some adult children, this is expressed in an expectation that Mom and Dad will fund portions of their lives. The signs that pop up at televised college football games reflect the cry of a generation, "Hi, Mom! Send money." In other children, it comes when adult children insist that their parents spend inordinate amounts of time helping them or caring for their children. Some parents feel trapped or overwhelmed by these demands. One young adult answered the phone to hear her mother say, "Honey, I am calling to see if Dad and I can bring your children by for you and Bruce to keep tonight. We have an invitation for a dinner date tonight." Obviously, this grandmother was wanting some relief.

And some parents may feel as if they neglected their children when they were younger, due to stresses of work or other factors. Parents who know that they gave their children less than enough time or attention may now feel the guilt of this neglect. Such guilt makes them less able to deal well with their adult children.

At the same time, some of those who need more from their parents stay away from home because they can't handle the complications of their families' lives. When Gary's son, Derek, was in the university, he remarked one Christmas: "Five of my best friends did not go home for the holiday. Their parents are divorced and they didn't want the hassle of trying to relate to them separately. They stayed on campus feeling as if they no longer had homes and families."

MORE ON THE MILLENNIALS

In this book we are talking about relating to your eighteen- to thirty-five-year-old child. Of course, some of the discussion will also help you understand and deal with older adult children, especially those Gen Xers in their late thirties and forties. But the focus is on those young adults who are members of Generation Y, or the Millennials or Mosaics—those born roughly between 1980 and 1995. While it may seem artificial and unfair to gather all Millennials into one pot, these young people do seem to share enough attitudes to make them a distinct group.

Knowing how great numbers of them think and feel can be helpful to you when you are at wits' end trying to understand your child.

This very large (75 million) generation has been described as optimistic, civic-minded, and socially aware—one author went so far as calling them possibly "the next Greatest Generation." However, they are also described as having a "sense of entitlement" and as "trophy kids" raised during a "child-centric" era, in contrast to Gen X, many of whom were raised as latchkey kids. Millennials may have overblown expectations for their work—when they can find work, which, as we have seen, is very difficult for many of them right now.

In work, school, and relationships, this generation tends to be more team oriented. They aren't just expert at technology—they take it for granted. They are comfortable with diversity. They are confident, but also very relational. And, say human-resource experts, they are hard workers. At the same time, while many were encouraged to achieve as they were growing up, they are less driven than their boomer elders.

Also, as we have seen, many of Gen Y are taking a long time to grow up. In previous generations, young people between ages eighteen and twenty-one were able to take responsibility for their lives. Generation Y, as Gen X before it, is maturing more slowly; we watch some of them beginning to take responsibility for their lives around age thirty.

The reasons for the longer maturing are not crucial, nor should our Generation Y children be criticized for the pressures (and diversions) that society and their parents may have given them. The point is their entry into true adulthood typically has been delayed. That raises a question. What is adulthood?

"EMERGING ADULTS"

In American society we used to have predictable times and means for marking the transition to adulthood, such as finishing high school, getting married, having children, owning a home, and settling into a career. But as Jeffrey Arnett, who coined the term "emerging adulthood," comments:

> To be a young American today is to experience both excitement and uncertainty, wide-open possibility and confusion, new freedoms and new fears.
>
> The rise in the ages of entering marriage and parenthood, the lengthening of higher education and prolonged job instability during the twenties reflects the development of a new period of life for young people in the United States and other industrialized societies. . . . It is a new and historically unprecedented period of the life course. . . . [that] should be recognized as a distinct new period of life that will be around for many generations to come.[1]

This is not the first time that the definition of "adulthood" has been adjusted in our society. When college or other advanced education became the norm for a large share of American men and women, the deferral of adulthood began. Young people delayed marriage, had their children when they were older, and started careers later.

Today as Millennials finish their schooling (and they are the most educated generation in our history), they are not always ready to tackle the challenge of jobs and families, a trend that has been developing for a number of years and has only been heightened by the recent recession. In their inability or reticence, as Arnett notes, they are creating a new phase of life between dependent childhood and independent adulthood. And, some see them as doing this on purpose. Career counselor Rebecca Haddock has noted, "Many of the students I work with are planning to return home after college. It's not viewed as a last resort. It's part of a plan."[2] Recent surveys have shown more than three-quarters of college seniors plan to live at home for a time.

These young people who move home can be divided into two groups: the *planners* and the *strugglers*. The planners expect to return home and to live there until they feel financially prepared to live on their own. The strugglers simply go home. They don't want to struggle alone and need the security of home.

A QUESTION OF EXPECTATIONS

What does everyone expect? Good question. What we have been talking about so far is the matter of expectations. We parents have some expectations that are very different from those held by our adult children. What we consider to be failure or immaturity may be regarded in a completely different light by our adult children. They may see their actions as careful planning, as normal and necessary steps in achieving their goals.

These differing viewpoints would not be so conflict-producing if our expectations were only for our own lives; but when our expectations lean on our children and seem to create pressures for them, trouble is just around the corner. And when our children expect certain things of us that we are not able or prepared to give them, we feel pressured. And then, when none of this is openly expressed, the pressure escalates and the stage is set for a confrontation.

Most parents, for example, expect some time for themselves when their children are grown. Instead they may feel put upon by their young adult children. Some parents watch as their children return home after college and take up residence in the home. When the adult children marry and do set up their own household, their parents may discover that the child care never ends. As one father said some years ago, "I thought that when the kids were grown, they would take care of themselves, but that isn't the case. When they marry and have children, my wife and I have that many more people to take care of." This particular family was very stable and loving and the father did not mean that the children were moving back home; rather, there was a level of emotional dependence he hadn't expected.

Parents also find themselves in confrontations with their adult children over other dashed expectations. Perhaps your children have given you disappointment, frustration, and concern from one of the following situations: doing poorly in college, wasting time and money; finishing college but then wandering and/or moving back home for a while to "get their feet on the ground"; having a marriage end in divorce in a few years, perhaps moving back home with a child or two; spending far beyond their means; or making lifestyle and employment choices that turn out disastrously.

A MORE POSITIVE FUTURE

In spite of profound changes during the past fifty years that have affected many families, we do see some hope on the horizon. Here in America we still have many parents and children who work through and enjoy their new relationships as the child becomes an adult. Many parents genuinely enjoy being with their adult children; several referred to their grown children as "good friends." And a variety of polls show that both the Millennials and Generation X want their marriages and families to succeed and "get it right" the first time, unlike their parents, whom they perceive as having rushed into marriages that later broke up. Like you, your children care about their future, and they are wrestling to know what to do.

Several authorities have been studying the impact of the Great Recession on Millennials. One 2010 study notes that while Millennials have been disproportionately affected by the Great Recession, they are "more upbeat than their elders" about their futures. The report also notes that there is less of a generation gap between Millennials and their parents than in past eras.[3]

It is these emerging desires in the hearts and minds of young adults that hold potential for a more positive future in marriage and family relationships. As parents of these young people, we must make every effort to assist them when they turn to us for help. We dare not ignore their desires.

when your
adult CHILD is not
SUCCEEDING

Barbara is very upset. Her twenty-two-year-old son finished college in May and spent the summer enjoying himself. It is now October and Phil is not looking for work. He spends his evenings hanging out with friends, arrives home after midnight, and sleeps half the morning. Some days he is still at home when Barbara returns from her office. When he is, they talk for a while and then he is off to see his friends.

Barbara was willing to accept his inactivity for the summer, thinking that perhaps he needed a break after his college years. But now that summer is long gone, she is very concerned. She often wonders what he is going to do; but when she asks Phil about this, he answers, "I don't know what I want to do." Once he talked about his friend Brian, who was teaching English as a second language in Budapest. He thought he might go and "hang out" with Brian for a while.

"Where will you get the money for that?" Barbara asked.

"I'll work. That won't be a problem."

Barbara took heart. But Phil hasn't mentioned Brian lately.

Barbara doesn't understand why Phil won't try to find a job so he can save money, get his own place, and begin to "get his feet on the ground." Anytime she talks to Phil about her expectation that he will move toward being independent, his response is unsettling.

"Why? Why would I want to tie myself down to a regular job at this point in my life?" he typically answers. "Maybe someday, if I ever have a family, but certainly not now. This is the time to hang loose, experience life, read, think, and meditate."

Barbara's husband left the family many years ago and Phil doesn't see him often. When they do get together, they end up arguing about Phil's future, especially since his father helped pay for college. For now, Phil finds it easier to stay away from his dad. He knows his mother has the same questions, but at least she isn't argumentative.

PARENTS IN A QUANDARY

Phil's parents represent millions of parents who just can't understand what is going on. They have loved their children and have done what they could for them within the imperfect circumstances of their own lives. And now that those children are seemingly adults, they are not living in ways that their parents consider adult.

If you find yourself in such a situation, you are having to deal not only with your child but also with yourself. If you take time to look inside, you will find some conflicting emotions that affect your relationship with your child. All parents have these mixed feelings to an extent, but for you just now they are heightened by the behavior of your child. In addition to the love and hopefulness you feel for your adult child, you also are experiencing some level of guilt and anxiety about your own role as parents. You may be asking yourself, "Is it my fault? Where did I go wrong?" You may even be thinking of some specific incidents and wondering if they were the catalysts that derailed your child.

Because these feelings of guilt and anxiety can complicate your relationship with your adult child, it is very important that you come to understand yourself and your emotions. Unless you deal with the anxiety and guilt, they will cause you more pain and confusion than you already have. And they may motivate you to take actions that you will later regret. This combination of guilt and anxiety can cause you to react inappropriately toward your adult child in one of two ways.

Becoming Permissive

The first kind of inappropriate response is to become very permissive. This happens when parents feel so guilty about past mistakes that they allow the adult child to manipulate them and to give in to unreasonable demands. Fred and Fran have one son, Tom. When he graduated from college, he took a job near the school, but he didn't enjoy it and quit after six months. He returned home and has been living with his parents for the past several months. Tom is not hostile to his parents and seems to like spending time with them. When they go out to eat, Fred, of course, picks up everyone's tab. And when Tom asks for money, Fred can't say no.

Both guilt and fear control Fred. He thinks that he was not a good father to Tom, and he fears that Tom will somehow reject him or will become depressed and discouraged if he doesn't give him what he wants. Fran strongly disagrees with Fred on this; she thinks Tom is quite capable of taking care of himself. She tries to convince Fred that he has been a good father and that he should not let his guilt feelings control his relationship with Tom. She also believes that giving in to Tom is not helping his self-esteem. In fact, the more dependent he is, the worse he will feel about himself. Fran finally persuades Fred to pursue family counseling so that they can learn to deal with their son in a more helpful and healthy manner.

Becoming Angry

The second way that guilt and anxiety can influence parental behaviors toward an adult child involves yet another emotion: anger. Fear and anxiety can cause feelings of anger. Guilt can easily affect the anger until it controls the parents' reactions of disappointment toward their adult child. Improper management of this anger can be harmful and even permanently destructive to the parent-child relationship.

John and Pam are parents to twenty-four-year-old Sandy, whose behavior is similar to Tom's. The difference in these families is that John becomes so distressed with Sandy's irresponsibility that he occasionally loses his temper and shouts at her, criticizing her inability to "get herself together." Of course, this hurts Sandy and breaks communication between them, often for days at a time. As John continues to vent his anger on Sandy, their relationship is slowly dying. Pam suffers immeasurably as she sees the growing distance between her two precious loved ones. This family also needs to seek outside help before the alienation gets to the point of no return.

It's crucial that we show self-control in our relationships with our adult children. This will enable our children to more easily communicate with us and will also provide a model of mature behavior. The better you do during this difficult time, the better your child will do. Your most important job just now is to maintain and attempt to improve your relationship with your child. Only in this way can you teach him to respect and love himself.

Showing Love

All of us suffer feelings of low self-esteem at times, but for our young adults between the ages of eighteen and thirty-five, these feelings can be very intense. In part they reflect a society that cares less and less about the individual. As parents, you are in the best position to help. You have the opportunity to influence your child for a lifetime; your love and emotional nurture can help your child move toward the maturity you long to see.

Simply loving your child during these agonizing periods is not permissiveness; you are not condoning her mistakes or failures. Loving your adult child unconditionally and unfailingly will help her resume her growth toward mature thinking and behavior. If you react unlovingly and unpleasantly, you are complicating everyone's life.

Be Objective, Not Emotional

In chapter 1 we talked about some of the characteristics of Generation Y. As you consider these characteristics (and others that you could add), you should try to remain objective in understanding the expectations your child has and the reasons why those seem so different from your own. An accurate understanding will help you keep your guilt and your anxiety in check. It will also enable you to maintain a greater evenness as you relate to your child.

It may also be helpful to remind yourself about the contrast between when you grew up and when your child did. Boomers lived through much social change, but there was still a perceived "norm" for work, family, and maturity. Society was much more uniform, technology much less advanced, and many people lived a more modest lifestyle than has been the case in recent decades, with the boom in consumer affluence. As well, there was more opportunity to secure a "good job" and provide for a family than there is today.

Generation X grew up in a very different world. Many of them came from single-parent families; from 1968 to 1977, both the divorce rate and the percentage of children born outside of marriage almost doubled, according to the U.S. Census Bureau. The Millennials have grown up in similar circumstances, although by the time they came along the divorce rate had somewhat stabilized and families had once again become more child-centered, even if those families did not look like the Cleavers. Many boomer parents sought to protect their children from perceived dangers in society—from increasingly negative media influences, and from unease about soaring crime and "stranger danger." The point is, today's young people have had to become experts in confronting change—in home, school, and society.

Be Optimistic

While your child has had to face enormous change, you may feel you have had to face the unexpected: an adult child who is immature and unproductive. You may wonder, *How? How can I help someone who acts like he hasn't grown up?* As family counselors, we have seen many situations in which young adults fell into disappointing behavior. In most of these, when the parents were loving toward them, the adult children were able to resume growth toward maturity and overcome their difficulties. (We also think of the response of Jesus of Nazareth, the first-century master teacher whose disciples showed anger, fear, and confusion. To them He gave His attention, understanding, advice, and love.) Parents with children in trouble or stuck in the pit of maturational process must remember that every such situation can be helped.

There is reason to be optimistic. Although adult children may seem to react negatively to every effort, they will eventually absorb their parents' love, hope, and optimism. They can change. Parents going through this kind of ordeal need to believe that God cares, and that He is especially sensitive to the feelings of hurting parents.[1]

HELPING YOUR CHILD FIND SUCCESS

Remember Barbara and Phil? They demonstrate the tremendous gap between the mind-sets of contemporary parents and their young adult children. Barbara sees the world through a traditional mind-set; Phil sees the world in a vastly different manner. His generation has been influenced to believe that there are no cultural or moral absolutes. To be rich is no more desirable than to be poor. To be married certainly does not bring more happiness than being single. Phil does want to be connected; that is why hanging with his friends is so important. But he doesn't want the responsibility of being tied down to one person, at least not yet.

How is Barbara going to relate to Phil in a constructive manner and not fall into the argumentative pattern that has developed between Phil and his father? Let's consider how she can deal with the tension that threatens to alienate her son and her. Doing so suggests several ways we can deal with our own children and help them to maturity and success.

Understand the Child's Point of View

First, Barbara must seek to understand her child's view of life. This requires a willingness to ask questions and then to listen with a desire to understand rather than judge. She is not likely to agree with Phil's philosophy of life, but she can understand it, if she will listen.

This is a bridge that many parents are unable to cross; they are so bound by their own outlook on life and what they believe to be best for their children that they find it almost impossible to see the world through the eyes of their children.

In reality, it is the parents and their peers who have created the mindset of Generation Y. These young people have looked at their parents' divorces and unhappy marriages and have concluded, "Why marry? It only brings great pain to the couple and to their children." It is not that the young people have a better way—they readily admit they don't know the answers. The question "What is the purpose of life?" still rumbles in the minds of Phil and his peers, but they are not sure there is an answer. That is why life for Phil and so many others is simply surfing, drifting, looking, thinking, and sometimes even hoping that they will make a significant discovery that will give life ultimate meaning.

If their parents are to play a positive role in their lives, they must first of all understand their children's viewpoint. We parents must recognize the child's perspective and admit that we are at least partially responsible for the problem.

Be Vulnerable and Real

Second, Barbara should be willing to be vulnerable, open, and real. When she does that—when any parent does that—she receives the child's respect and often the right to be a mentor. Barbara already feels that she has been vulnerable, but this is going to call for an even larger dose. She and all of us with children in this stage need to admit our own frustrations and disappointments with life and acknowledge that we have made some poor decisions. Being honest in our own struggles with life's meaning is a prerequisite to effectively giving any insights we believe will help our children in their search for meaning.

It's been a long time since parents were able to operate with the attitude that "Father—or Mother—knows best." Young adults are not convinced. We must join them as fellow pilgrims rather than speak down to them from a position of superiority. Our children can and will dialogue with us as they do with their peers if we are willing to create the same nonthreatening and nonjudgmental atmosphere.

It is not that young adults are not looking for guidance. They do want advice, encouragement, and support, but from people they respect. If we parents are to serve as their mentors, we must remove the barriers that have been built in the past and then learn to communicate, not as all-knowing parents but as individuals still in the process of learning. We need to share our thoughts as ideas rather than dogma. When our children see us as helpers rather than controllers, they are more likely to be influenced by our ideas.

Recognize That Your Vision Differs from Your Child's

Third, Barbara needs to accept the reality that her visions of what Phil ought to do are not his visions. She needs to respect Phil as an individual and give him the freedom to think thoughts, dream dreams, and view life differently than she does. According to the Judeo-Christian worldview, this is what God does with us. He gives us the freedom to think our own thoughts and make our own decisions, even when they are not in keeping with His.[2] This does not mean that our thoughts are as valid as God's. It does mean that God values human freedom and does not wish to treat us as robots.

Parents who want to relate to their young adult children in an authentic way should remember that truth: each person has distinct thoughts and the right to make decisions in his or her way. Our children's vision of the future and their choices in the future are theirs to make, and we must respect those choices, even if our children must suffer consequences of wrong decisions.

Begin an Honest Dialogue

Fourth, Barbara can begin an honest dialogue with her adult child. By giving Phil the freedom to dream and choose, Barbara has opened the door for dialogue. She can now discuss with him the implications of choices within that framework and talk about where certain courses of action may lead. She may share examples from her own experience, since she is not using them as a club but as a flashlight to identify the realities in the path ahead.

For instance, she could now discuss with Phil the question "Do you think I am helping you or hurting you by allowing you to live here with me without paying any rent or contributing to other expenses? I am not asking this to manipulate you but in an honest effort to help both of us think about what is best for you." Such a question and the ensuing discussion may well lead to a meaningful look at the purpose of food and its importance. If it is valuable to eat, then what must one do in order to get food? The connection between work and food becomes obvious. This may even lead to the axiom written to a first-century church, "No work, no eat."[3] In such a conversation, Phil may realize that his lack of work, far from enhancing his own self-worth, is in effect destroying it.

If Barbara moves to the question "What do you think Brian is getting out of teaching English in Budapest?" chances are that Phil's answer will include the satisfaction in helping others. They are now discussing the idea of finding one's significance through service. This is a theme that runs through the pages of all great literature and that should resonate with Millennials. It may well be the motivation Phil needs to add a dimension to his life other than "hanging out with his friends."

Such a dialogue is usually effective. It communicates respect for your adult child's opinion, helps you understand him better, and can help him sort through options. We recommend your pursuing a dialogue whenever possible; it is always preferable to a one-sided lecture.

Consider "Tough Love"

What if Phil is not motivated to find work? Barbara may need to try another approach. She may need to employ "tough love." If she is convinced that her financial support to Phil is to his own detriment, and if she has seen no movement toward getting a job, she may well say, "Phil, I've been thinking about our conversation some weeks ago. I've come to believe that I'm doing you a great disservice to let you continue to live here with me without making any financial contribution. I think this is fostering your dependence on me and is hindering you from developing an independent lifestyle. Therefore, starting next month, if you want to continue to live here, I'll expect you to pay $200 for housing and $200 for food. Of course, if you want to make other arrangements, I'll understand. I just believe it is my responsibility to do what I can to help you develop an independent lifestyle."

You may need to consider a tough-love approach. At times tough love can accomplish what tender love will not. Remember, tough love is still love. Though the child may suffer (for a season) from your withholding aid and permitting adverse consequences to come, the purpose is loving: his maturing by learning and acting independently. Keep in mind, though, that tough love is used only after other more congenial approaches have failed. It is not the place to begin.

OTHER ISSUES TO ADDRESS FOR SUCCESS

Not all young adults are characterized by an "anything goes" philosophy. Many of them have been raised in traditional (and often religious) homes, and they hold to traditional values. Yet they too can and at times do struggle with the move to adulthood. Their apparent lack of (or limited) success is due to various causes. These adult children may do poorly in school, work, or family and social relationships. The parents may bemoan their seeming immaturity.

When you discover the cause(s) of the poor performance, you can help your children take appropriate steps. Three reasons an adult may struggle are: (1) low self-esteem; (2) a rebellious spirit; and (3) poor academic or emotional background.

Low Self-Esteem

Low self-esteem is a common emotional malady, affecting many young adults. Our culture has exalted the beautiful, the intelligent, the athletic, and the talented. Yet, most of our population does not fall into these categories. Consequently, thousands of young people are plagued by feelings of inferiority and even worthlessness when they compare themselves to their peers. These inner feelings of insecurity often keep them from reaching their potential in school, at work, or in human relationships.

You can detect if this is the case for your child by listening to what he says. Such statements as "I'm not sure I can do it," "I'm not as good as Trent," "I'm afraid to try," "I just can't get it," or "I'm not cut out to be a student" are telling you that the problem may be low self-esteem.

A Rebellious Spirit

Some young adults fail to achieve because they are angry with their parents and are subconsciously trying to hurt them. Psychologists commonly call this *passive-aggressive behavior.* Because they seem passive on the outside, their parents don't often observe the anger or rage that lies beneath. But the children's behavior is showing that it is there.

By his action or lack of action, the rebelling young adult is saying, "You will not control my life. You will not tell me what is important in my life." The harder the parent presses this child to be successful in school or in other areas of life, the more the child will resist.

ACADEMIC AND EMOTIONAL PROBLEMS

Other young people perform poorly at work or in school because they do not have sufficient background academically or emotionally to handle the requirements. Someone who makes A's and B's in most subjects and D's in another may not have the background to understand the concepts and do the work. The same thing often happens in the workplace, especially where technical abilities are required. These young adults may be passed over for promotions and eventually lose their jobs if this inadequacy is not taken care of.

More adult children attend school and enter the workplace with disabling emotional problems, including anxiety, depression, poor motivation, and problems in relating to others. The culprits include the many destabilizing trends in our society, such as divorce, poor parenting, and poverty. Even crime and sensational entertainment in movies, television, and online contribute to fear and confusion.

These problems have become so common that they are sometimes seen as normal. Many people today need help in these emotional and relational areas. Some young adults desperately need good mental health services in order to adequately function in society—services that increasingly have been curtailed by managed-care programs.

CONVERSATIONS AND COMMENDATIONS

Unless you discover the reason for poor performance, you will not be able to help your child. The primary means of discovering what is going on in your child's life is to communicate, to have conversation as a peer rather than as a parent. Taking a judgmental attitude, complete with verbal tirades, simply puts more distance between you and your child. It is far more productive to ask sensitive questions designed to help you understand what she is thinking and feeling. Then wait for her to ask those little words "What do you think?" before making suggestions. Unsolicited advice will almost always produce a negative response. But, when your child feels that you genuinely care and understand, she is far more likely to receive your counsel.

Just like everyone else, young adults welcome words of encouragement. When we are troubled by their poor performance, we need to look for areas that deserve commendation. Our tendency too often is to say nothing about their small successes because we feel their potential is so much greater. But affirming their small accomplishments tends to motivate a more positive response. In contrast, condemning words tend to generate negative feelings.

If you conclude that your adult child has low self-esteem, encouraging words will be especially helpful. "You've done a nice job fixing up your room. It really looks nice" is certainly to be preferred to "Why are you still painting your room? You should be looking for a job." Similarly, "That's a nice song—I like the rhythm" is better than "Why are you on the drums? You should be studying math." Young adults tend to perform best in areas in which they have a personal interest.

When we commend our children's successes in key areas (even though those areas may not be important to us), we create motivation to succeed in other areas. When we condemn their efforts because we think they should be spending their time and energy somewhere else, we create a negative climate and emotional distance between us. The ancient Hebrew proverb is true: "The tongue has the power of life and death."[4] Affirm your children, and they may feel renewed zeal to succeed and try again.

when the NEST isn't EMPTYING

We noted in chapter 1 many changes that make being a parent of a young adult now far different than being that parent in 1961. Among the many changes during the past fifty years, none has affected parents more than the not-so-empty nest. Adult children used to leave the home "nest" shortly after finishing high school. By 2008, fully 77 percent of graduating college seniors planned to return home to live with their parents for a time. This trend has been growing for a couple of decades—even in the early 1990s, 55 percent of young people ages eighteen to twenty-four were living with parents.[1]

As common as this arrangement is, however, it is still difficult for many of the midlife parents who were looking forward to having more time for themselves and each other. Although they expected to feel a brief time of loss after the children left for college or work, they still anticipated their increased freedom.

The reasons for staying with parents often make sense, though they don't lighten the parents' duties. Today the primary factor, of course, is economic. But even beyond financial factors, in a society of fewer shared values and greater ideological conflict, many young people feel anxious and pessimistic, and they want to extend the transition to adulthood and independence. For other young adults the high cost of higher education keeps them homebound. Today more and more students are attending local colleges and continuing to live with their parents. Or, they may go to their state university but return often—to eat Mom's cooking and to do their laundry. Once they are in college, they expect to be treated differently at home, wishing to come and go as they please. They have people to see and things to do, and they don't plan to spend a weekend at home visiting with their parents. At the same time they are continuing to make the home nest a very busy place, they are taking on average two years longer to finish their college degrees.[2]

THE NESTING SYNDROME
Should the Nest Empty Immediately?

Judith Martin, the formidable syndicated columnist Miss Manners, suggests that we might do well *not* to believe some parents when they complain about their adult children staying at home. She thinks their groans are merely "conventional."

> Too modest to brag that people who know them only too well actually want to live with them, [these parents] claim that the attraction must be free or cheap board and services. Others may be saying this to protect their children from worse outside attacks. Few people hesitate, when they hear of such a situation, to express the modern assumption that adults who live with their parents are financial, romantic and psychological failures, unable to get decent jobs, stingy, emotionally stunted, lazy, irresponsible, bad marriage prospects, self-indulgent, and afraid to face the world.[3]

Miss Manners is puzzled that our society should consider it normal for parents and children to want little to do with each other, and feels that a child's resulting flight from home is "an unseemly display of family disloyalty."[4]

We acknowledge that the extended time together can be a very positive experience. It provides young adults a needed and limited period of time to prepare themselves for independence. This is especially important if they value the quality of their family life and find strength and encouragement there. Home becomes a place of shelter for those not yet able to deal with the anxieties they find in an uncertain world, as well as a place where grown children can start to get on their feet financially. For parents who find it hard to part with their children all at once, the additional time their children live at home provides them a valuable transition.

Yet, having said all this, it is true that many parents have questions about the nesting syndrome, especially about their roles and attitudes. Even those who find the experience generally positive wonder at times if they are being too permissive and soft with their children. They don't know what limits and rules are appropriate. Also, they don't always know how to handle the changing expectations of their children in relation to them. Other parents are uneasy about having their children stay at home, while some are openly angry at what they regard as an imposition.

If you are a not-quite-empty-nester, you know that you are dealing with a complicated mix of expectations and emotions that are not going to go away or resolve themselves. You may also be perplexed about the best way to handle your situation. Regardless of the varying expectations of parents and young adult children, almost everyone can make a continuing nesting experience a growing and exciting adventure for the entire family. We are not saying it will be easy, but, as in all relationships, a little work will pay off in huge dividends.

Even if your adult child remains at home, keep in mind that you are still parenting, although in somewhat different ways. As in all parenting situations, you want to do all you can to give your child your love and care, regardless of the stress you or your child may be feeling. It is also important that you stay clear of two parental traps: authoritarianism and permissiveness. If you can do this, while at the same time refusing to give in to negative feelings, your child will come sooner to maturity and independence. Make your home atmosphere as warm, upbeat, and supportive as possible, a place for making positive memories for everyone.

Families who have lived through the unempty nest may feel tensions but also reap rewards. Meet two families, the Colliers and Petersons (all names are changed), who have grown through the adult children's presence in the home.

What the Colliers Learned

Neal and Deb Collier have been married for twenty-eight years and have two children. Their son, Adam, is twenty-three and a third-year student at the local technical institute. He lives with his parents. Adam tried one year at the state university but dropped out during his second semester because he was failing three subjects. His failure was due to two factors: lack of good study habits and a propensity to party rather than study. He came home, regrouped, took a summer school course in study skills, and for the past three years has done fairly well in school. His sister, Jessi, is twenty-one and a sophomore at the state university, majoring in art history. She comes home every two or three weekends; sometimes she brings a friend but usually comes alone except for her dirty laundry and her pet hamster, Herman.

Jessi always lets her parents know a few days ahead when she will arrive home. Deb prepares one of Jessi's favorite meals for Friday evening and Adam arranges his schedule so that they can catch up on each other's lives. Their dinner conversations sometimes continue for two and three hours, as they talk about the books they've read, movies they've seen, and what is happening with their friends. As part of the conversation, family members share their weekend plans. When they all have plans, Friday evening and church on Sunday may be the only time they are together.

If Jessi wants her parents' help on a school project, finances, or her car, she lets them know by phone or email. She does her own laundry, and sometimes she and her dad take a walk before she returns to campus on Sunday afternoon.

Adam has a steady girlfriend and his parents always make her welcome in their home and often take the couple out to eat. When Adam moved back home, his parents made it clear that they were happy to have him, and that they wanted to help him get a college education if that was his choice. They also acknowledged that things would be different now that he was out of high school. His room would be his room, which meant that he would take the responsibility for keeping it clean—to his satisfaction, not theirs. He was welcome to have guests over, but not overnight. (One of their friends had been caught running a free "boarding house" for all their son's friends, and they did not want to get caught in this trap.) Adam's schedule is so different from that of his parents that they can go a day or two without seeing each other and often leave text messages as to their whereabouts. Neal and Deb have agreed that as long as he is in school, they will pay for his car insurance and will not charge him any rent. When he finishes school and gets a full-time job, if he chooses to continue living at home, he will pay a monthly rent and take over his car payments and insurance. For now, he has a part-time job that pays enough to cover his gas and food away from home. He and his folks eat together on Wednesday evenings, either at home or at a restaurant.

Such "rules of the road" are not uncommon when parents let their adult children remain at home. The rules may include policies regarding payment for rent and/or food and specific duties and expectations. (More on this in chapter 4.)

Neal and Deb's home is not an empty nest, but neither is it a place of conflict. If they have a problem with Adam or he with them, they call a family conference and discuss it openly. In three years they have had only two such conflicts and have resolved them in a friendly fashion. They all enjoy this "unempty nest" stage of life. The children often ask their parents' advice about school and also their relationships. Deb and Neal feel that they are giving their children the freedom to develop their own independence and at the same time continuing to have a positive influence on them.

What the Petersons Learned

John and Sherry Peterson have a different sort of unempty nest with three children at home, and they too have managed to make it good for everyone. Seventeen-year-old Jill is a junior in high school; she plans to train later to become a nurse. Rick is nineteen and doesn't have a job. Marc at twenty-one is the assistant manager of a local store. Neither Rick nor Marc wants to go to college.

Since graduating from high school, Rick has had three part-time jobs but quit each one to take a trip with his friends. He has no particular vocational interests; he does plan to work but hopes it won't interfere too much with his life. Marc had worked in a grocery store during high school and became friends with the manager. After graduation he set his sights on becoming a store manager. Within three years he made assistant and is thoroughly excited about the possibilities.

When Marc decided not to attend college, his parents were disappointed. Neither of them had gone and they hoped all their children would. When Rick, their second born, announced that he also had no interest in college, his parents were more disturbed. Unlike Marc, he had not worked part-time during high school and after graduation it took him three months to find the first of his part-time jobs. With his record of quitting jobs, his parents were concerned about his future.

When Marc decided that he wanted to work toward becoming a store manager, John and Sherry called a family conference to let him explain his desires to the entire family. The conference included not only his career plans but negotiations about continuing to live at home and how this would impact the rest of the family. They discussed Marc's ongoing contribution toward family chores.

When they came to the matter of finances, Rick spoke up in defense of Marc not having to pay any rent, since he would be saving for his own place.

"I understand," Dad responded, "but on the other hand, isn't that part of what it means to be an adult? That you begin to pay your own way? When one is young, parents take care of all a child's needs, but when you get to be an adult, you begin to take care of yourself."

Marc agreed with his dad and said he preferred to pay something toward household finances. Mom suggested that they begin by charging a relatively small amount that would increase by $25 a month until it reached the same level as if he had an apartment of his own.

Sherry had another concern about Marc's staying home, one especially important to her. She said, "I'm afraid that if we agree that Marc can come and go as he pleases, I am going to be staying awake at night wondering where he is if he doesn't come in by, let's say, midnight. Being his mom, I just can't help it. I want him to have freedom to do what he wants to do, but I also want some peace of mind myself. You know, Dad and I are adults, but we don't come and go without telling each other where we will be. Because we are part of the family, we let one another know if we are going to be late or if something unexpected arises. Part of being a loving family is that we do not cause each other concern."

That conference took place three years ago. Marc is still at home and is now paying $675 a month for rent and utilities. Their plan has worked well and neither he nor his parents have any complaints.

Ah, you say, *so a family conference with members agreeing to rules is part of the solution.* Yes, but a conference will not always satisfy everyone. With Rick the situation was somewhat different and led to another family conference. Although John and Sherry were concerned about his lack of direction, they understood his desire to travel, since they wished they had done this when they were young. They agreed to one year for travel, after which Rick would go to school or get a job. He was also in a band that played at local events and this kept him out very late, sometimes all night at a friend's home. Sherry wanted to know where he was, and Rick agreed to call whenever he wouldn't be home for the night, even if it was well after midnight.

When they got to the subject of finances, they realized that he wasn't earning what Marc had right out of high school. Rick felt he should not pay, yet his parents thought that he should pay a small amount of rent, just on principle. Jill and Marc also agreed, though Marc noted that while traveling, paying rent would be difficult and unfair for his brother. After much discussion, their father said, "What if we say that when you are on a trip with your friends, you won't pay any rent. But when you are living here, for one year, you will pay $25 a month. That's minimal, to be sure, but at least it lets you make a contribution to the family."

Rick agreed to that and also to Jill's request that he do household chores when home. Then their father added, "I think we should understand that we are all agreeing to this for only one year. If you should decide to continue to live here after the year, then I think we will have to take a fresh look at all of this." Again, Rick agreed.

After one year of relative freedom, Rick began to consider what he would do. He has been very good with computers for many years and thinks he may go into sales. His parents feel quite comfortable that he will settle down and do well in whatever he chooses. Now that the year of travel is past, they have made it clear that he must either go to school or to work. They are not open to him continuing to live at home for $25 a month. If after he gets a job he wants to continue to live at home, they all agreed that the plan they followed with Marc would also be a workable plan with Rick.

Meanwhile, in another year Jill will begin her training to become a nurse and the family is committed to support this ambition.

John and Sherry are pleased with the relationships they have with their young adult children. They feel they have been successful in making this extended nesting period a productive time in their own lives and the lives of the adult children.

GUIDELINES FOR THE UNEMPTY NEST

These two families highlight several guidelines for relating to your young adult children still living at home. The foremost of these is that as a parent you *clarify expectations*. If you have one set of expectations and your older teenager has another, you are all setting yourselves up for a battle. But, if you can all agree on the expectations, you will be laying a foundation for a harmonious relationship now and in the future.

Here are five other guidelines for the home that hosts adult children:

1. Maintain open communication. You cannot clarify expectations without having open communication. We strongly recommend the family conference illustrated by John and Sherry—an open forum where each family member can share ideas and feelings and together come to a consensus. If you have used this approach in earlier years, you know its benefit. If you have not, this is an excellent time to begin. In this type of open forum, you as parents need to listen carefully to the thoughts, feelings, and desires of your children. This does not mean that they have the final word, but that you take their opinions seriously.

2. Balance freedom and responsibility. Every parent is challenged to help the child find the proper balance between freedom and responsibility, since they are two sides of the same coin. In dealing with children who may not feel very much like adults yet, you need to keep in mind that you are all trying to arrive at appropriate guidelines. Certainly emerging adults should be given more freedom than high school students, but freedom does not preclude responsibility. If they are to live at home, they must assume responsibilities for the welfare and peace of the family. These need to be made specific in areas of finance, chores, and common courtesies.

3. Honor your moral values. Moral values have to do with actions we believe to be right and wrong. Frequently the personal values of young adults differ from those of their parents. If your adult children plan to continue living at home, you have a right to ask them to continue to respect the values of the parents, at least while they are in the home. It is certainly appropriate for you to say that your children are not welcome to invite persons of the opposite sex to spend the night in their rooms. It is also appropriate to expect that your young adult children will not use tobacco, alcohol, and drugs in your house, if these are your values. In so doing, you are not forcing your personal values but expecting your children to respect your beliefs as long as they live with you. A kind but firm commitment to your own values demonstrates that you have strength of character.

4. Consider your own physical and mental health. When Sherry insisted that Marc and Rick let her know where they were late at night, she was protecting her own health and well-being. She knew that she would lie awake worrying if she didn't know their whereabouts. Some parents are able to disconnect and let a young adult come and go as he pleases, while others are not. Most parents want to know when the adult child will return; otherwise they worry for his or her safety. If that's your approach, set an appropriate rule that everyone lets others know when they will be back at night. You need to know your own limitations and take care of yourself responsibly. You cannot help or influence others if you don't first care for your own needs. This may even touch on the state of a child's room—sometimes closing the door is better than looking at a mess.

5. Set time limits and goals. When John and Sherry agreed to allow Rick to travel and have a year of freedom after high school, they were letting him do something valuable but with a time limitation. Also, their agreement with Marc about paying increasing rent defined his financial responsibility to the family. Setting a goal regarding when the adult child will move out can give him motivation. The limits may vary. If engaged, the child perhaps can stay at home until the wedding date. If he has an entry-level job, perhaps the family agrees the child will move when he gets his first promotion. Often the parents and young adult find it easier to agree on a definite time limit, such as six months or one year. While goals and time limits may need to be renegotiated along the way, it is important to have them in place from the beginning.

DISORDER IN THE NEST

As you read about life in the Collier and Peterson households, you may have wondered, *Is it always this perfect? Where are the arguments? This isn't what happens in our house.* We acknowledge that ongoing nesting arrangements aren't always positive and enjoyable for everyone. You may be in an uneasy situation that you wish would end.

When parents and their young adult children share the same roof, tensions can develop for many reasons. The parents may feel they have lost their freedom, and the child may feel he is not respected as an adult. Both parent and child are adults with their own preferences. Each may have the desire to control. The kitchen, den, and bedroom can all become battlefields. The phone, television, and shower may be sources of irritation. This often leads to arguments. In fact, the primary complaint of most parents in your situation is that there is too much arguing in the home.

That may be true, and it does no good to assign blame for who's causing the arguments, your child or you. More important is what you can do to reduce the arguing. Because your young adult child is still dependent on you, you may be tempted to respond to disagreements the same way you did when your child was much younger. You may say something like "I'm still in charge here. This is my house and I say how things are going to be!" This sort of response may sound and feel good at the time, but the result will not be positive in the long run. Being unpleasant to your child will get you nowhere. Dumping your resentment or anger on your child will cause him to resent you. This only provokes another argument and another.

When tensions escalate during an argument, you may be at a loss as to how to handle the situation. You may even feel so upset that you fear you will lose control and say something that will truly cause harm. And yet, you have to say or do something. Please remember these two words: *pleasant* and *firm*. If you can be both pleasant and firm, you will get through the tough time without doing damage that you will have to apologize for or repair later.

The most mature stance for parents is to *refuse to argue*. It is not always easy to gain enough self-control to do this, but it pays off in countless ways. The key is to listen to your child's side of a situation and then use "I" messages, which calm anger and invite understanding. A "you" message begins with the word *you* and generally sounds accusatory and unpleasant. "You make me so angry when you do that!" An "I" message conveys your feelings and expectations but does not lay blame. "I really feel angry when you do that." No one can argue with how you feel. Such messages will help you to remain pleasant but firm—and they will help your child understand what is causing your feelings of anger.

DEALING WITH THE ANGER

Remember that as a parent you have the greatest influence on your children, for good or bad. The factor that has the most influence on them is the way you manage your anger. The way you manage your anger affects your children's: (1) self-esteem; (2) sense of identity; (3) ability to relate to other people; (4) perceptions of the world; and (5) ability to manage stress and function in society.

If you mismanage your anger, you can cause your children to develop attitudes that are: (1) passive-aggressive; (2) anti-authority; and (3) self-defeating.

When you manage your anger in a mature fashion, you give your children one of the most caring gifts there is—a potent example that will help them grow to their own maturity without the afflictions that so many adults struggle with today. It is wonderful to see your children develop into conscientious, energetic, motivated, and well-liked adults, but this process takes time. And Generation Y seems to be taking its time in reaching maturity. The way you handle your anger will have a tremendous influence on how well and how fast your children mature.

The reason that parental management of anger is so important is that children of all ages are so sensitive toward their parents' anger. It is impossible for them to pass it off or to take it casually. Even one incident of mismanaged anger will cause extreme pain, just as mature handling of anger can intensify the love between parents and children. Every day you have a choice as to how you will handle your emotions in relation to your children. If you behave in a mature way, you will strengthen your bonds in the family.

As we all know, we can be well-intentioned regarding our emotional reactions, and then be caught off guard by an unexpected turn of events. This is what happened to the Athertons and their nineteen-year-old daughter, Nina. When she graduated from high school, she decided to live at home while she attended college. She was in a co-op program that offered her part-time work during college years and a good opportunity for employment after college.

Before Nina was far into her studies, her father began having acute difficulties at work. Jim's company was downsizing and his job was on the line. This caused tension not only on the job but also at home. He and his wife, Joan, were already feeling financial stress due to a poor investment that Joan had warned against from the beginning. Now as the tension increased, Jim became more and more depressed, withdrawn, and anxious. As a result he was very short with Nina and would frequently scold her for minor misunderstandings. He quickly went from being anxious to showing anger.

Nina withstood her father's unreasonable confrontations, but before long she dreaded coming home. When the home atmosphere worsened, Nina moved out of the house.

Because she wasn't ready for this financially or emotionally, she was unable to keep up with her work/study program. She became depressed and was not able to function well. Fortunately, Jim and Joan recognized their daughter's declining health and were able to get her and themselves into counseling, where they came to realize how they had failed their daughter. At this point Jim was laid off, but he and Joan handled themselves well through it all and were able to give Nina the emotional support she needed. They persuaded her to move back home and they worked at learning how to handle their anger and frustration in appropriate ways.

Nina said that two things helped her through this hard period. First, "My dad realized that I needed him. I also was sure that he still loved me." Despite his own agonies, Jim was able to keep her emotional love tank filled during that troubling time. Second, Nina felt that her faith in God sustained her, especially when things were at their worst. Before Jim and Joan got the help they needed, Nina felt completely abandoned and alone, even in her prayers. But later she said, "God did answer and He brought something wonderful out of a miserable situation. The Lord is very good at this sort of thing!"

TECHNIQUES FOR MANAGING ANGER

Everyone gets angry on a regular basis. Therefore, the question isn't whether you will become angry but how you will manage the emotion when it arises. The following suggestions for dealing with your feelings of anger will help you with your young adult children and also in other arenas of life.

First, *take responsibility.* The first step in managing anger is a willingness to be responsible for it. It is so easy to blame someone (or something) else for making you mad, and then to hold the person responsible for what the anger "made" you do or say. Unfortunately, many people use their anger as an excuse for whatever they want to justify. Consciously or unconsciously, they seek reasons to get angry so that they may excuse their own wrongdoing!

Before you can take responsibility for your anger, you need to identify it. As family counselors, we often see people who feel jealous, frustrated, or hurt and who are not aware that the basis of these feelings is anger. Although these people may not be aware of their anger, their children surely are. When parents refuse to identify and deal with their anger, their children feel less respect for them. However, when parents identify the anger, they are then able to name it and admit, "I am angry." Only then can they assume responsibility for it.

Blaming a child for your anger is self-defeating. It is also dangerous, because you will naturally blame her for other angers caused by totally unrelated situations. For example, you may have had an unresolved disagreement at work that you "forgot." When you come home, your adult child's behavior upsets you. If you blame her for your anger, you may also unconsciously blame her for your earlier encounter at work. This sets you up to dump accumulated anger on the child. This tendency to dump anger is a common problem most parents have as a child emerges from a dependent state to a more self-sufficient state.

Second, *remember the anger.* Because you don't feel proud of yourself when your anger gets out of control, it is easy to "forget" what happened. It is crucial to remember how you behaved, or you are later likely to unload your anger on someone else, or oversuppress it and become passive-aggressive. So after your feelings subside, recall them. Remember your actions and their effect on others, as painful as that may be.

If this is a problem for you, we suggest that you keep a notebook of your progress in coping with anger. For instance, if someone treats you unfairly and you feel deeply hurt (angry), you may not be in a position to confront or deal with the hurt. But you can log the incident in your notebook and later record how you resolve the problem. The best way to handle the anger is verbally, pleasantly, and directly with the person you are angry at. If possible, you want to move toward reconciliation and greater understanding between you.

Third, *keep yourself healthy.* The better your general condition physically, spiritually, and emotionally, the more effective you will be in handling anger. Your body needs a balanced diet, and much information exists on nutrition in our diet-conscious society. This does not mean you must reduce weight or try to eliminate your intake of fat. One little-known study has shown that too low a level of fat in the diet can cause anxiety and irritability. It is generally recommended that fat in the diet should be about 30 percent of the total caloric intake.

Reducing the calories may be appropriate, however. Millions of Americans are becoming increasingly overweight and out of shape, which can lead to depression and, in turn, anger.

Fourth, *use self-talk.* Even though you try to manage your anger well, at times you may lose it and risk dumping on your child. What then? One valuable technique is self-talk. Tell yourself something like, *I'm losing it. I don't want to make a fool of myself and say something I will later regret and have to apologize for. I'd better cool it!* If that doesn't do it, you might add, *I don't want my children to rebel or develop into irresponsible people. I had better behave myself and be a good role model.*

If the self-talk doesn't calm you down, leave the room, start some chore—anything to get alone so that you can think about the situation and why you got so angry. It may help you to remember a funny or endearing incident involving your child, one that will bring up pleasant feelings. What you are really doing is taking a "time-out," just as you had your child do when he was small.

Fifth, *ask forgiveness.* If you have said or done something that you regret, you have a great opportunity to let good arise from a bad scene. The simple but difficult act of asking your child's forgiveness puts your relationship back on a loving basis. Regardless of the immediate response, this act enhances the child's respect for you and teaches your child the importance of forgiving others and oneself.

Since you got into the conflict in the first place, don't be afraid to constructively resolve it by asking for forgiveness and then moving toward a better relationship. Never forget that true intimacy comes from resolved conflict.

You can bring good from your painful encounters as you and your child move toward greater maturity and understanding.

when your CHILD moves HOME

Y ou may have seen the T-shirt that says, "It's not an empty nest until they get their stuff out of the attic." For you that may not seem even remotely funny. You aren't thinking about emptying the attic but about how you are going to manage when your child moves himself and all his things back into your house and life.

The Mitchells knew this all too well. As Jan explained to Dr. Braun, a family therapist they were seeing for the first time, "This is the last place we ever thought we would be. And to get Greg here is a near miracle!" Her husband nodded his head and then explained why they had come to the counselor.

"Our kids have always done fairly well. No serious problems—just the usual stuff. After they finished college, we thought our parenting days were essentially over, but were we ever wrong! Our second child, Nick, graduated from a good university and was ready to get out on his own, or so we thought. He took temporary jobs and lived with friends for nearly a year, while he was looking for a position related to his field of study. When that didn't happen, he became discouraged and asked if he could move back home."

"What could we say?" continued Jan. "He just wasn't making it out there. He felt like a failure and seemed to lose all motivation. We had never seen him that way before and so we let him come home. However, that made us wonder if we hadn't done a good job as parents. Nick has been home now for three months and just sits around the house. One day we think maybe we should just let him rest and recover and the next day we feel like wringing his neck and pushing him out the door. We're on an emotional roller coaster—we're worried, frustrated, and scared."

"Whenever we talk to him about it," said Greg, "he just looks at us with forlorn eyes and tries to be agreeable, saying something like, 'I'm trying, Dad,' or agreeing with whatever we say. Then he goes to his room or watches TV. He hasn't even looked for a job except online in the usual places."

Dr. Braun asked the Mitchells to describe Nick's high school and college experiences.

"He was always an easygoing kid who kept up with his friends. He was active in sports and a leader in church youth activities," Jan said. "He got above-average grades without studying too much. He seemed to feel reluctant to leave home for college but soon adjusted to life there. He did fairly well in college, was involved in some activities, and dated now and then, but nothing serious. He graduated not knowing what he wanted to do, but that's not too unusual today. I guess he figured something would just pop up. When it didn't, he asked to move home. Tell us, did we do something wrong as parents?"

Before Dr. Braun could answer, Greg asked his own question: "Why isn't he out there doing his thing? When we were his age, we couldn't wait to get away from home and make our own way. What's wrong with him? I know times are hard, but still . . .

"Maybe we did too much for him. Maybe we didn't teach him to be responsible," Greg went on. Jan leaned toward her husband and said, "Now, don't blame yourself. We need help for Nick; that's why we're here."

"But we've hardly gotten started, Jan. We haven't told Dr. Braun about Jennifer."

"She's older than Nick?"

"Yes, she's twenty-eight and has a three-year-old daughter. Last week she and little Ava moved home and this is what really prompted us to seek some help. Her husband of five years was killed in a traffic accident a few months ago, and they didn't have enough insurance for her to keep the house they had just purchased. She just sold the house and needs our help for a while.

"She was always very responsible, did well in school, got a nursing position after college. However, she has worked only part-time for the last four years and feels that she needs a few more courses to get back into a changing medical scene. We understand her situation and are glad to help her. What we don't understand is our own reactions. We dearly love our granddaughter but we hadn't counted on taking care of her this much, or on having our two children back home at this time in our lives."

"BOOMERANG KIDS"

You may know a Nick and a Jennifer in your home or just down the street, for their numbers are increasing. As we said earlier, it isn't the fact of two generations living in the same house that causes the problem, but the unexpectedness of the return home. The boomerang effect: You think they are gone and then they come back to you. That's why when adult children come back home, they're often called the boomerang kids.

Responding to Their Return

As Jan and Greg learned, their main problem was not the return of the children but their own reactions and uncertainties. After the Mitchells were able to better understand themselves and also work out practical ways to deal with Nick and Jennifer, their anxieties lessened. The parents and the two adult children all were able to enjoy this unexpected time together again, and now with Ava too.

After Jan and Greg had met with Dr. Braun several times, they told Nick that they wanted him to come along with them to several sessions, since what they were discussing involved the entire family. When he resisted, they used the leverage they had hesitated to use before and told him that since he was living there, he needed to work toward a solution of the problem that sent them to the therapist in the first place. When Nick realized he didn't have much choice, he accompanied his parents to several sessions with the therapist.

To his surprise, Nick found the conversations helpful in better understanding his own fears and lethargy and also in understanding his parents' feelings. It wasn't long before he began seeking jobs and giving serious thought to what he wanted to do in the future.

Since Jennifer's move home was beyond her control and was to be for a limited time, and since she was pursuing advanced training to enable her to reenter nursing, Jan and Greg decided to relax and just enjoy the time with their granddaughter.

Responding to Emotional Issues

Young people return home for several reasons—some practical and financial, but some emotional. And there are times when parents have reason to be concerned about the emotional health of their children who bring with them the scars from their unsuccessful attempts at making it in the adult world.

Rose was one such person. At age twenty-nine she returned home, her self-confidence shattered by her experiences of the last ten years. Her father, Will, told the counselor he contacted, "We have a serious problem on our hands. Rose has returned home with real emotional problems, and we don't know how to help her. We don't mind her living with us for a while, but we know this is not good for her in the long run."

Dr. Clark agreed to see Rose the following week. When she came to the appointment, he saw that she was very self-effacing. She apologized for being late, even though she was two minutes early. During the conversation, she said "I'm sorry" numerous times, apologized for taking his time, for crying, for using his tissue.

Rose's ten-year journey from the nest and back had been mostly a downhill slide with only a few intervals of temporary excitement. She remembered the thrill of going off to college, but she remembered even more deeply the lonely weekends when other girls were dating and she was in her room or in the library. She made good grades and was commended by the professors, but she had few friends.

Rose received her bachelor's degree in economics, and soon after college got a job in the business office of a local company. She moved into her own apartment. Her work went well, but she had little social contact. Then she became active in the singles program of a large church. She attended their social occasions and enjoyed doing service projects with the group. During the next years, a few young men asked her out, but only one of them called a second time.

Then she became good friends with Martha, and the two decided to live together and share expenses. This was a happy period in Rose's life, since the two women had many common interests. "We really enjoyed being with each other," Rose told Dr. Clark. "But Martha began dating seriously the next year and, of course, we spent less time together doing things. A year later, Martha married and moved out of town.

"I really was happy for her, but it hurt me. I felt a sense of loss when she left."

As she talked, the counselor learned Rose felt depressed. Others in the church group had tried to encourage her by inviting her to various events, but her depressive behavior pushed them away. Finally, Rose dropped out of the group.

Her depression also affected her work to the point that her boss suggested that perhaps she should look for another job. This was the last straw for Rose, since the job had been her one place of stability and achievement. "I felt like an utter failure. Three months later they let me go. I just didn't have the heart to look for another job, so I asked my parents if I could move back home."

Rose is typical of many boomerang children—they return home the worse for wear. Their experience in the adult world has depleted their emotional energy, and their psychological and physical problems motivate them to retreat from life rather than pursue a vision. Parents who open their doors to these tired children are often tired themselves. They don't have the skills to cope with their young adult children, and in an attempt to do so, they often become frustrated and depressed.

Rose's father acted responsibly when he reached out for help within a few weeks of her return home. He and his wife were willing to provide her a place to stay but they were unable to deal with her emotional and social problems. In promptly seeking help, he was admitting his own limitations. This is an important step in responding to boomerang children. Many parents fail to take action, hoping that their child will soon regain emotional composure and reenter the adult world of independent living. Months can drag into years of the adult child becoming more dependent.

For Rose, help came soon. In addition to providing counseling for her and her parents, Dr. Clark was able to get Rose enrolled in a class on building self-esteem where she learned some valuable concepts and also found new friends. When the class ended, she took another on building relationship skills. In this one she learned why she had been unable to form long-term relationships in the past. With the help of the group and individual counseling, she was able to correct many behavior patterns that were barriers in her social contacts.

Within three months of returning home, Rose had another job and nine months later she moved into an apartment that she would share with another young lady. Her depression had lifted and she was excited about the possibilities of the future. That was five years ago. Today, Rose has been married for two years and is expecting her first child. She looks back on the year she spent with her parents as a critical turning point, a time in which she dealt with problems she had never faced before, and took personal steps of growth to overcome destructive personality patterns.

PLANNERS AND STRUGGLERS

In chapter 1 we briefly mentioned two types of returnees: the planners and the strugglers. In this section we want to look at the characteristics of these two groups in some detail.

Differences between Planners and Strugglers

Planners intend to spend the time at home in preparation. Their rationale usually includes saving money, paying school debts, and building a nest egg for the future. They see their parents' home as a sheltered and inexpensive environment while they seek the perfect job and spouse.

Yes, these people may seem to be maturing slowly, but the planners are usually savvy in the way they use their resources to their advantage, often without being a burden to their families. Even if they don't hit the right career track right away, they are still working, and many of them contribute to household expenses.

Evidence indicates that planners generally do well in moving home and preparing themselves financially and socially for a secure future. They add vitality to their parents' lives, and their relationships with family usually thrive and deepen with mutual respect and understanding.

Strugglers tend to return home out of necessity. Their plans go no further than "living at home for a while." They find the outside world threatening and don't want to struggle on their own. They do not see the world as their oyster and do not want to leave the security of home. They are simply not ready for the intense competition and rapid change of today's society.

Young adults who are strugglers have many motivations. Most of them are normal adults who are slow in their maturational process. If they are handled well by their parents, they will reach the level of maturity necessary to go out on their own and lead productive and meaningful lives. They simply need more time in the nest. Parents who can respond with understanding will later be delighted and overwhelmingly proud when their children become independent adults.

Forming New Bonds

Parents who have adult children at home can consider themselves fortunate in several ways. First, they are able to help their children; many parents lose close contact with their adult children. Parents of strugglers also have the opportunity to rectify past mistakes and to escape the dreadful feelings of guilt that plague many parents, sometimes for the rest of their lives. With these returning children, parents can form new bonds of love and affection while strengthening old ones; this can create some of the most meaningful memories between parents and children.

Another positive is that parents have additional time with their children while the children are developing life's values. For example, twenty-two-year-old Bobby has returned home having spent four years in college, but without completing his degree. He is now looking for work and wondering what to write on his job application. Does he put down "graduated from college" or "attended college"? *Won't the latter raise unnecessary questions in the mind of the hiring manager? Will the employer actually check my college records?* These questions of expedience versus integrity race through Bobby's mind, and he decides to discuss the issue with his parents. His parents have the opportunity to help Bobby consider the importance of integrity. At this crucial stage in his life, their influence can affect his success or failure for years to come. If he were not living with his parents, Bobby may never have discussed the issue with them, and they would not have had this opportunity.

Most strugglers who come home need emotional support, and this can place their parents in a difficult role. The strugglers have met with failure or experiences they could not handle. They are hurting and need love and support. As parents we must remind ourselves that we *all* need our parents' love and support. After a parent dies, we need the memory of their care and love.

In a time of stress it is easy to forget these truths. When a struggler returns home, we must not lose the overall picture of family ties over a lifetime. If we fulfill our parental duties to the best of our ability, we will see our adult child heal, recover, and fly again. At the time, it may seem like a nightmare, and we may feel betrayed as we watch our own offspring appear to fail. Yet, we can also see it as a wonderful opportunity. The future is not dark. Our adult child will heal, regain his strength, and try again. Isn't that what life is all about?

BEING LOVING . . . AND CHALLENGING

When an adult child is experiencing hardship, disappointment, and pain, the way her family and loved ones treat her will make the difference in the character she develops. If she is treated with respect, encouragement, love, and support, she will eventually come out of the difficult days a more mature and capable person. But if parents treat her with dismay, frustration, and anger, she will suffer even more and most likely become a bitter person with more pain to overcome.

Parents need to maintain a balance as they seek to help. First, they should offer support in their love, encouragement, and perhaps financial help. And second, they should challenge the adult child to assume responsibility for herself and become an independent person. Because challenging the adult child is more difficult to negotiate, we want to offer guidelines for getting through it successfully. It is important that parents and the adult child come to agreement about these items. Here are three ways to be loving yet challenging to your adult child:

1. Establish a time limit for the nesting experience. This does not have to be totally rigid or inflexible but there should be some sense of how long the arrangement will last. Everyone will feel more relaxed if they know there is a time limit. (See chapter 3, page 48 for strategies for setting the limit.)

2. Formulate a financial agreement that will take into account the financial goals and situations of all parties, as well as the expectations of all. In the rare event that a young person cannot make any financial contribution to the household, he can make other contributions, such as cleaning, yard work, repairs—anything that will aid the household.

3. Respect the need for privacy. The amount of privacy people need varies greatly, and this difference can become a source of friction and misunderstanding. This is an area in which open communication pays big dividends.

WHEN ADULT CHILDREN
RETURN WITH THEIR CHILDREN

Often boomerang children return home bringing their own children. When this happens, their parents' stress level may skyrocket. Not only do they face the pressures of dealing with their children, but they have the logistical and emotional struggles of caring for grandchildren. George and Shirley found themselves in this situation. When their daughter Beth returned with two young children, she told her parents that her husband had been physically abusive for the past five years and now had left with a woman he met at work. Beth was furious with Stan and also at herself that she had allowed the abuse to go on for so long.

Her children were bewildered at what had happened to Daddy. They were excited about staying with their grandparents but they often asked, "When is Daddy coming?"

George and Shirley opened their doors and their hearts to Beth and her children. They knew this was going to cause a radical change in their lifestyle, but they saw no alternative at the moment. They were not in a financial condition to rent an apartment for Beth; also, they knew that she needed their emotional support during this crisis.

During the first week Beth was there, her parents suggested that the three of them sit down and talk about the situation and decide on a strategy. George began by saying, "Beth, I want you to know that we want to do everything we can to help you through this crisis. We know that this is not what you wanted, but it's where we all are and we have to deal with it. If we are going to be successful in coming through this crisis, we have to work together as a team. Why don't we begin by making a list of the areas we'll need to deal with in the coming months?"

Together they made the following list:

Child care
The children's physical and emotional health
Food preparation
Finances

Beth's emotional health
Legal matters related to Stan
George and Shirley's emotional health

"There are probably other things, but that is enough to confront now. Why don't we take the ones that seem most urgent and then talk about the others next week," George said. "What is most pressing on your mind, Beth?"

"It all runs together for me. I know that I must take care of the children, and that's a full-time job. I also feel strongly that Stan needs to be held accountable for his actions. He needs to pay regular child support to help us financially. I guess those are the two biggest things on my mind now."

"Then let's discuss those two today," suggested George.

They agreed that in the coming week they would try to find a lawyer for Beth so that she could begin the process of holding Stan accountable for helping the family. They also agreed that Beth should get some counseling to help her process her emotions. Shirley, who had a part-time job at the library each morning, would be willing to keep the children on the afternoons that Beth needed to be involved in legal proceedings or with the counselor.

For the next several weeks, they continued to have family conferences dealing with various aspects of their life together and one by one worked out agreements for handling the logistics. Three months into the process, they decided that within a year Beth should plan to have her own apartment with the children and also a part-time job. With this income and the money she hoped to receive from Stan, she could be self-supporting.

Fifteen months later, Beth was able to move into her own place. She had found a job that she could do from her home. The children went to preschool each morning, and George and Shirley agreed to keep the children two nights a week to give Beth some time to see friends.

UTILIZING COMMUNITY RESOURCES

When struggling adult children return home, many parents are not able to manage the problems alone. It is important to be very open to finding and using services offered by people in the community. Counselors, ministers, and physicians all stand ready to give individual attention. Local colleges, social groups, libraries, churches, and other organizations often sponsor activities designed to give practical help to those struggling with emotional, financial, or physical difficulties. Parents who encourage their returned children to utilize these resources provide a great service for their young people and also for themselves.

This is particularly important in families having children with some form of handicap. Adult children with disabilities pose special challenges. As institutions that serve persons with disabilities continue to close, the number of people living at home rises. This can be a draining and ongoing experience for parents. Their children need continuing help, but so do they.

In addition to the many professional people in the community whose job it is to serve such families, most churches are willing to help, if they know how and when. The parents are the ones who know best what would serve their family, and they should feel free to make reasonable suggestions to the appropriate persons at their churches. We have all read wonderful stories of handicapped individuals who are vitally involved with people in their neighborhoods, but such involvement has to be coordinated by a caring person, usually a parent, who enlists the help of those who want to serve.

WHEN PARENTAL PATIENCE
ISN'T ENOUGH: SAYING GOOD-BYE

When children return home, parents need to remember that they are adults and ultimately responsible for their own lives. All the planning and goals and support and resources available will not do the job if the young person isn't amenable to change. If they choose to walk away from parental love and support, they have that freedom.

However, in some cases they don't walk away; instead, they stay too long. When a boomerang kid refuses to leave, his parents are in a difficult position. They know he is able to take care of himself; he seems to have recovered from his bad experiences, and is generally pleasant. Yet he refuses to take responsibility for himself.

Ryan, twenty-eight, was still living at home. He had spent his college years studying minimally, making poor to fair grades, and had not graduated. He would get excited about an area of study, take a few courses, and then lose interest. Although he was capable of excellent work, he always seemed to find ways of failing to meet the expectations of parents and teachers alike. Ryan was a social butterfly with many friends and didn't seem to have the time or inclination to work for more than a short time.

His parents finally insisted that the three of them go for family counseling where they had regular sessions for six months. During this time it became increasingly evident that Ryan was not going to cooperate or attempt to become a self-sufficient person. His father, Jeff, wanted to tell him to leave home, but his mother, Lucy, was unwilling to be that "cruel." As they talked with the counselor, they agreed on a plan that satisfied Jeff's need to take action and Lucy's need to be gentle.

Ryan's parents laid out a plan for him. They would set him up in an apartment and pay his living expenses for six months. After that time, they would decrease the support so that he would be on his own in six months. Although this was risky, Jeff and Lucy felt that they had no other option.

Ryan was livid and began to accuse them. "You really don't care about me! Decent parents don't kick their child out on the street. I'll never forgive you for this. You'll be sorry!" His anger nearly caused Lucy to back down, but she was finally able to see that Ryan's response indicated that he really did need to learn some lessons in the school of hard knocks, just like everyone else.

When his anger didn't work, Ryan tried to negotiate with his parents, promising that he would do better in school and take more responsibility, if he could just stay at home. Jeff reminded him that he had said those same words at other times, but without honoring them. All of this was very difficult for Lucy, but deep down she knew that their plan was best for Ryan.

When he saw that he had no other options, Ryan moved out. And gradually he changed. He found employment that would meet his financial obligations if he trimmed his lifestyle. Eventually he learned to be responsible for his way of life. Now, he is thankful to his parents for being firm with him.

At times, parents will have to act, giving a deadline and then enforcing it by asking the adult child to leave the home for his own welfare. This is love—tough but true love—in action. Often this action can be preceded by counseling.

LOVING OUR BOOMERANG KIDS

As you well know, boomerang children can present you with a wide variety of challenging situations that call for adaptability, imagination, innovation, firmness, love, and every other skill you ever learned in your many years of parenting. You met the challenges of the past and you have to believe that you can also meet the ones confronting you today. The goal is to move your children to maturity and to let them eventually be free of the home nest, out on their own.

Most boomerang children respond positively to the love and encouragement of their parents. They are at a point of crisis and know they need help. They have returned to the one source where they believe they can receive such help. As they and you keep the future in mind, you can all proceed with optimism. You and your children are going to be connected in vital ways as long as you all live; you want to move toward their future, and your own, with skillful and loving care that offers promise of what you all want most.

major HURDLES
to INDEPENDENCE

A lex was an outgoing young man, well liked by almost every-one who knew him. Bright, good-looking, and talented in many areas, Alex took his first position with a manufacturing company immediately after college graduation. He liked the job (it was related to his area of study), and he did very well at first. After six months, he received a good evaluation and a bonus. His parents were pleased for him.

However, a year later, Alex's attitude was changing. He began to be irritable when asked to do something requiring extra effort and started complaining to fellow employees about the company. When he missed meetings or came to work late, he made excuses. As the quality of his work diminished, the more important work was given to other employees. His boss did everything he could to help Alex, spending extra time with him to encourage him. He even changed his responsibilities, giving him work that he thought Alex would enjoy more. Nothing seemed to work, because Alex always found a way to fail.

When eventually he was fired, he complained bitterly that he had been wronged. He threatened to sue the company and called an attorney.

As the two talked, the attorney told him that he had no basis for a suit, but Alex did not believe him.

Alex managed to be hired by another company, but he displayed the same kind of behavior, and within two years he was terminated there also. After a third such failure, Alex returned home to live with his parents.

They were bewildered but supported him in the best ways they knew and had a surprisingly good relationship with him. Eight months later, Alex was still living at home and making little effort to find another job. His parents managed to persuade him to seek help from a counselor well versed in depression and anger.

Alex faced and overcame two of the most common hurdles to our children reaching independence. In this chapter we will look at four major hurdles to our children leading full, mature lives. And we will see how we as parents can help them reach maturity.

THE GOAL: INDEPENDENCE

As parents we want our children to reach the point where they can function independently of us. We want this for their own good and also for ours, since we have been through many years of the hard work of parenting and now desire the freedom that comes with the empty nest. Parenting has wonderful rewards but it also requires an exacting price. We have all heard grandparents say, "We love having the grandchildren here, but we also love to send them home."

Having done the hard work of parenting, we look forward to the time when we can enjoy the fruit of our labors, watch our children follow their own dreams while we explore new horizons for ourselves. It is the way life is designed—children are born to become adults.

If all goes well, we will encourage our children through the uncertain years of young adolescence, watch them grow in self-confidence through their high school years, reach out to pursue education or vocation, eventually support themselves and probably a family, and continue to relate to us in a positive but somewhat less intense manner.

However, in contemporary Western culture, it is a common story for an adult child to have a history of doing well in life up to a certain point and then begin to have problems that cripple him to the point of devastation. Alex had that happen to him, but with firm, loving parents and a willingness to accept counsel, he changed. Most adult children in similar predicaments can receive the help they need and go on to enjoy a happy and productive life, since most of the problems are quite treatable, if they are identified and treated in time.

Since parents are usually the ones observing their children most closely, they tend to know when something is beyond the range of ordinary and needing special help. And yet, many hesitate, because they do not know the signs by which to identify potentially serious problems. As we discuss four of the most common hurdles to independence and offer guidance to parents, we encourage you toward the goal: to bring your children to maturity and independence.

The four hurdles we will consider are depression, anger, alcohol and drug abuse, and attention deficit (hyperactive) disorder (ADHD).

DETECTING DEPRESSION

Depression is the most common problem that can harm or destroy a young person's life. Not only is it a malady in itself, but it complicates all other difficulties. Remember Rose, who fell into a depression when her roommate left and Rose felt she had no friends? Her work suffered and eventually she "felt like a complete failure."

Although depression today is more recognized than in the past, it is still one of the most unrecognized causes of problems in young adults. Depression in young adults is very similar to adolescent depression, and that makes it complex, subtle, and dangerous. It is complex because of its many complicated causes and effects. It is subtle because it almost always goes undetected, even by the young person, until a tragedy occurs. It is dangerous because depression can result in the worst of happenings—from work failure to suicide.

Severity of Depression

In this age group, depression is hard to identify because its symptoms are different from the classic symptoms of adult depression. For example, a young adult in *mild depression* usually acts and talks normally and gives no outward symptoms. Mild depression is manifested in depressing fantasies, daydreams, or in dreams during sleep. It is detectable only by knowing the person's thought patterns and thought content. Not many professionals can identify depression at this stage.

The young adult in *moderate depression* acts and talks normally. However, the content of his speech is affected, as he dwells primarily on subjects such as death, morbid problems, and crises. Since many adults today seem to dwell on pessimistic trains of thought, the child's depression may go unnoticed.

Moderate depression in the young adult is just as profound and serious as moderate depression in the older adult. Biochemically and neurohormonally, the two are identical, but the manifestations and symptoms are usually different. A moderately depressed older adult looks terrible, feels miserable, and is severely affected in his ability to function. At the same level, the young adult does not appear depressed. Therefore, when a young adult seems to others to be extremely depressed, we need to assume that he is profoundly depressed and in real trouble.

If the depression deepens, a *severe depression* can develop. The mental and physical pain at this stage can be excruciating, even unbearable; yet the young adult will still try to mask the depression. But there are certain telltale signs, which we will discuss shortly.

One reason depression is difficult to identify in young adults is that they are good at masking it. They can cover it by appearing to be all right, even when they are absolutely miserable. This condition is often called "smiling depression." Young people unconsciously employ this front, especially when other people are around. When they're alone they let down the mask somewhat. This letdown is helpful to parents, who are then able to observe their children when they believe no one is looking at them. The transformation in the face is amazing; when they are alone, they appear terribly sad and miserable. As soon as they think someone is watching, they assume the smiling mask.

As a concerned parent, you will want to know how you can discover depression in your child so that you can do something about it before a tragedy occurs. A depressed young adult is quite susceptible to unhealthy peer pressure, and is prone to fall victim to drugs, alcohol, inappropriate sexual experiences, and other self-destructive behaviors.

Symptoms of Young Adult Depression

The best way for parents to identify depression is to recognize its symptoms and how those symptoms develop. It is crucial to be aware of all symptoms, since one or two may or may not signify true clinical depression. True depression is a biochemical and neurohormonal process—yes, it affects the body's blood chemistry and hormones—and usually develops slowly.

A depressed young adult will usually have at least one of the symptoms of older adults. These include feelings of helplessness, hopelessness, despondency, and despair; problems with sleep (either too much or too little); problems with eating—too much or too little, with weight loss; and lack of energy. Other symptoms can be feelings of low self-esteem and problems handling anger. It is important to remember that depression causes anger.

Now, let's look at specific symptoms of depression in the young adult:

• **Shortened attention span.** In mild depression, the first symptom generally seen is a shortening of attention span. The person is unable to keep his mind focused on a subject as long as he once could; as his mind drifts from what he wants to focus on, he becomes increasingly distracted. This shortening of the attention span usually becomes obvious when he attempts to do detailed work or read complex material. He finds it harder to keep his mind on the subject, and the harder he tries, the less he accomplishes. Of course, this leads to frustration, as he blames himself for being stupid or dumb. He assumes that he does not have the intellectual ability to do the work, and this is damaging to his self-esteem.

• **Daydreaming.** The shortened attention span affects the adult child at work. At the beginning of the day, she may be able to pay attention, but as the day goes on, her short attention span becomes more noticeable. As her depression deepens over time and the attention span shortens, her daydreaming increases. Unfortunately, this is usually interpreted as laziness or poor attitude.

• **Poor work performance.** As the attention span shortens and daydreaming increases, the result is poor performance at work. Naturally the person's self-esteem suffers and this causes the depression to deepen even further.

• **Boredom.** As the young adult daydreams more and more, he gradually falls into a state of boredom. This usually manifests itself in his wanting to be alone for increasingly long periods of time. He also loses interest in things he once enjoyed.

• **Somatic depression.** As the boredom continues and deepens, the adult child gradually slips into moderate depression. At this point, she begins to suffer from *somatic depression,* that is, bodily depression. We use this term because even though depression is physiological, or has a bio-chemical-neurohormonal basis at this point, the symptoms begin to affect the person in a directly physical way. For example, in moderate depression, the young adult begins to experience physical pain. This may occur in many places, but is most often felt in the lower mid-chest region or as headaches.

• **Withdrawal.** In this miserable state, the adult child may withdraw from everyone, including friends. And, to make matters worse, she doesn't simply avoid her friends, but may disengage herself from them with such hostility, belligerence, and unpleasantness that she alienates them. As a result, she becomes very lonely. Since she has so thoroughly antagonized her good friends, she finds herself associating with rather unwholesome peers who may use drugs and who may be in trouble.

Once prolonged boredom has set in, other symptoms can develop. The mental and physical pain at this stage can be excruciating and at times unbearable. A young adult in severe depression cannot tolerate his misery indefinitely and eventually becomes desperate enough to do something about it. At this point, drug or alcohol abuse may occur, or sexual adventures or sexual fantasies through pornography. Complete withdrawal from others is one telltale sign of severe depression.

Most amazing at this point is that many young adults are hardly aware that they are depressed. Their ability to hide behind denial is truly incredible. This is the reason that others seldom suspect their friend—or child—is depressed until tragedy occurs.

Moderate to severe depression is not something you can consider a "phase" that will run its course. This insidious affliction tends to grow worse and worse unless the depression is identified and intervention is taken.

The struggler is more likely to be affected by depression than the planner, but depression can occur with any adult child. When it happens to young adults, it can affect their chances of making a start in the world, finding the spouse best for them, getting into satisfying activities, and making friends. It is often the underlying reason why an adult child returns home and becomes a boomerang kid.

At one time or another, depression affects millions of people in the United States—a governmental estimate places the number at 1 in 20 Americans.[1] Parents must be able to recognize the symptoms of depression if they wish to help their children.

Different Causes of Depression

It is also important for parents to realize that there are different kinds of depression and that they come from several causes. Depression may be a by-product of a *serious physical illness.* Also, it may be *situational or reactive,* in that it grows out of a painful situation in life. Such depression is a reaction to difficult experiences, especially those that involve loss. For example, depression often follows the loss of a spouse by divorce, the loss of a job, the loss of a parent to death, the loss of a friendship, or the loss of money. Depression may also arise over the loss of a dream.

Another form of depression is rooted in a *biochemical disorder* that puts the mind and emotions in a state of disequilibrium. This is sometimes referred to as *endogenous depression,* meaning "from within the body."

The good news about biologically caused depression is that it is readily treated with medication. The bad news is that only about one-third of all depressions are biological. Situational depressions are far more common and medications are of little or no value in treating these, unless they have gone on for a long time and have affected the body's biochemistry.

HELPING WHEN YOUR CHILD IS DEPRESSED
Foster Communication

What can a parent do if a child is depressed? The first thing, of course, is to identify the depression before it becomes severe. Once it is identified, parents can do much to help, even though they are in a difficult position, as most depressed persons are difficult to communicate with.

With this inherent hesitancy to communicate, the parents must try to keep open or reestablish the lines of communication. Badgering a child with questions is usually an exercise in futility, since the young adult is not far removed from the depths of adolescence and may tend to react like an adolescent. Trying to get her to talk may increase her defensiveness.

So what can you do to foster communication? If your adult child is content to be in the same room with you, as you both read or work on your laptops, you are fortunate. Simply being in the vicinity of the depressed young person is a form of communication. It gives you the advantage of taking your time and making sure that you do nothing to cause her to put up more defenses. You can wait until your child takes the initiative to open or continue communication. It is good to let her bring up what is on her mind, what is troubling her. When this happens, you can offer suggestions about the underlying depression. It is best to approach this rather delicate subject when your child asks for your opinion. Most adults are touchy about their mental health and will accept suggestions only when they ask for them. If you have a good enough relationship to be able to be near your adult child at times when she is relaxed, you are in a good position to talk to her about your concerns when she is ready.

If such an opportunity does not present itself, you may wish to create one. One possibility is to take your child on a trip or some venture where you will naturally spend time together. Even if your child doesn't broach the subject, you may bring it up, using "I" messages such as, "I hope I'm not imposing, but I would like you to know of my concern for you." Such a statement has the best chance to be taken positively and get a favorable response.

Your child may respond with slight hostility—for instance, "What do you mean?" If she does, you can still continue the conversation. As long as you remain pleasant and soft-spoken, the interchange will continue until she understands that you care about her happiness and are worried that she may be depressed.

The main reason you want to be so careful about the way you approach your child regarding her depression is that you don't want her to misinterpret what you are saying. Also, you want to elicit her cooperation in finding help. This may be in the form of a competent counselor, the use of an antidepressant medication, making constructive life changes, or all of these. The important thing is to maintain a positive relationship with your child during this difficult time.

Recognize the Dos and Don'ts of Depression

Most parents are not able to give their children the kind of specialized help they need, but they can encourage them to find the professional assistance that will help. As parents are in this delicate position of urging without pushing, they may be guided by the following suggestions:

Dos
- Do tell him that you are glad he is going for counseling.
- Do let him know that if he wants to talk, you want to listen.
- Do receive his feelings without condemning them. If he says, "I'm feeling empty," your response might be, "Would you like to tell me about it?"
- Do look for life-threatening symptoms such as suicidal talk or actions.

- Do inform the counselor of such talk.
- Do tell her that you believe in her and know she will come out of this.
- Do encourage her to make decisions, but don't force her.

Don'ts
- Don't tell him that he has nothing to be depressed about.
- Don't tell him that everything is going to be OK.
- Don't tell him to snap out of it or pull himself together.
- Don't tell her that the problem is spiritual.
- Don't tell her that the problem stems from her past failures.
- Don't tell her why you think she is depressed.
- Don't give advice; rather, encourage her to listen to her counselor.

Remember, you can encourage your child; you can be supportive and create a climate for healing, but you cannot be the therapist. With proper help, your child will likely work through the depression and be able to move toward independence.

ANGER AND PASSIVE-AGGRESSIVE BEHAVIOR

Our nation has significant problems with anger. From "road rage"—people using their cars as weapons (or firing guns from their cars at offending drivers)—to verbal or physical abuse in homes (upwards of four million women are seriously beaten by partners each year), violence occurs on all levels of American life. There are many forms of anger, but the type of anger that causes the greatest problems, especially for teens and young adults, is called *passive-aggressive behavior*. Like depression, it is a behavior that is seldom identified.

A Definition

First, a simple definition for an often misunderstood term. Passive-aggressive behavior is primarily a subconscious determination or motivation to do exactly opposite of what one is supposed to do. Typically the behavior opposes what an authority figure wants done; the angry individual intends to upset or anger the authority figure.

Passive-aggressive behavior is the worst way to handle one's anger because it is a choice to do wrong and can become part of one's character. Although it begins as a subconscious choice, it can to some extent become conscious. If passive-aggressive behavior is not understood and dealt with, it can harm and even destroy a person's life.

That's what almost happened to Alex, who lost three jobs and then returned home to live with his parents. As we noted, his parents, believing he was angry and depressed, convinced him to receive counseling. After extended time together, the counselor concluded that Alex was indeed clinically depressed and angry. She was able to help him leave both these barriers to becoming a mature adult. The counselor was able to convince Alex that he indeed was handling his anger in passive-aggressive ways. She also found out he was clinically depressed, and the depression increased the anger, aggravating the acting out of his anger passive-aggressively.

There's a happy ending to Alex's story. The counselor treated the depression first. As it responded to treatment and his anger subsided, she was able to teach Alex how he was failing to manage his anger maturely, and was using passive-aggressive behavior as a way of handling his anger.

It took Alex and his counselor more than a year of working together to make good headway. He is now able to understand the underlying cause of his puzzling behavior and is continuing to make progress in controlling it. Passive-aggressive ways of handling anger are difficult to treat, but persistence will pay off. Therapy is usually the only approach to treating it.

Recognizing Passive-Aggressive Behavior

Now that you have seen an example of this behavior, we need to show you how to recognize it in those you know. There are three signals that suggest this behavior. First, the child's behavior does not make rational sense. It made no sense for Alex to fail in the workplace. He had everything he needed to succeed — he was trained in that field and was initially competent. Even when he tried to do well, he subconsciously managed to act out against authority, without understanding his motivation in doing so.

Second, you can suspect passive-aggressive behavior when nothing you do to correct the behavior works. Remember, the purpose of passive-aggressive behavior is to upset the authority figure; therefore, the child will resist all your efforts as one in authority to change him or her.

Third, even though the purpose of passive-aggressive behavior is to upset the authority figure, it is the passive-aggressive person who actually gets hurt and suffers the ongoing consequences. Alex's behavior was subconsciously designed to upset the employer, but it was Alex, not the employer, who suffered the consequences. Unless he changes his immature way of handling anger, Alex will continue to manifest it passive-aggressively with family members and future employers. He will likely have problems with spiritual authority also.

If your adult child is handling anger passive-aggressively to such an extent that it is hurting her, you will want to find a way for her to get the help she needs. Counseling is important, but timing is crucial. She must be at the point where she genuinely seeks ways to change her behavior.

If you are feeling your adult child's behavior is illogical, rebellious, and self-destructive, it may be he is displaying passive-aggressive anger. And you may need to act not only for your child's welfare, but for your own.

ALCOHOL AND DRUG ABUSE

The Impact of Substance Abuse

Alcohol abuse and drug-related problems have become a national scandal. Whatever we have been doing for the past fifty years in prevention and cure is not working. Alcohol and drug abuse may connect with some of the factors we have talked about in this and other chapters, a primary means of coping with the pressures of being a young adult. Researchers have found that among young adults "excessive use of most kinds of drugs is higher than for other age groups in the population."[2]

Although alcohol is reported as being beneficial to health in limited quantities, we know that even a small amount of alcohol can cause radical changes in personality and behavior. In larger quantities, it can have harmful and even destructive effects, physically and psychologically.

Similarly, some prescription drugs and others sold over the counter are habituating. If your adult child has an ongoing prescription for a painkiller or sedative, watch him and be aware of the medication's addictive properties. If you believe your child is addicted to a prescription medication, notify his physician. When such drugs are taken with alcohol, they are even more dangerous and can lead to death. Both nonprescribed and prescribed drugs used not according to directions—that is, abused—will have harmful effects over the short and long term, as will the abuse of alcohol.

Some short-term effects are drowsiness, poor coordination, impairment of judgment, and decreased reflexes. Long-term effects can be permanent problems with memory, and damage to the liver, brain, vascular system, and central nervous system. There is little doubt that abuse has wreaked havoc among a segment of adult children who return (or stay) home as they support an addiction or lose a job because of an addiction. Often they are skilled at hiding their substance abuse.

You may dismiss this as a possible reason for your adult child to be at home, or you may believe your child is addicted and want him to leave your home. Let's recognize, though, there are reasons our children may fall into a substance addiction, and a compassionate but firm response is in order. First, as the stress in our society increases, the use of drugs also increases. That's a key reason drug and alcohol abuse continues to thrive among our hurting young adults. Stress causes fear, anxiety, depression, tension, nervousness, and dysphasia (becoming unable to use or understand language). When these become unbearable, as they do in some people, drugs can induce pleasant-feeling states such as relaxation, calmness, euphoria, power, and invulnerability. As the pace of life grows more hectic, and as our society becomes more impersonal and alien, those most vulnerable will experience a loss of control over their own lives because of their extreme anxiety. In an intense and fast-paced social climate, chemicals present a very real temptation.

Responding to Substance Addiction

When parents realize that an adult child has a chemical problem, they are often the ones who will have to initiate some sort of intervention or suggest treatment. However, they are in a difficult position because their child may deny having a problem. A daughter may say she only drinks "on occasion" and can put the bottle or glass down whenever she wants to; she may envision an alcoholic as someone who is in a continual stupor, which she clearly is not. It is easy for the abuser to drink enough beer to qualify as an alcoholic but still assume that she is fine, because one glass of beer is relatively low in alcohol content. All persons who drink have their own idea of what is an appropriate amount to consume. However, most communities have information centers where you can find out what qualifies as alcoholic rather than social drinking. You can also find out about treatment possibilities and groups such as Alcoholics Anonymous, and Al-Anon and Alateen for family members.

Drug users also can be creative in denying their problems. Your son may admit to using marijuana but say, "I'm not taking the hard stuff like cocaine, and I don't plan to." Or he may say it is only for "recreational use," is relaxing, and won't lead to addiction. As we noted, drugs can produce pleasant feelings of relaxation, calmness, and euphoria. But they also enslave, creating a dependence for false, temporary feelings of comfort.

Here are three specific ways you can help if you suspect that your child has a chemical dependency problem. This is the best advice we can give: Seek counsel from a qualified person on what steps you should take. Handling such a situation yourself is extremely difficult and sensitive, and it is so easy to make a bad case even worse. You want to avoid being in the position of provoker or enabler. Second, seek encouragement through prayer. Remember, God still answers prayer. He can guide you to the best sources of help and also to the best attitudes and actions that will benefit your child and your entire family.

Third, practice "tough love." This tough love means letting your adult children suffer the consequences of their drug and alcohol abuse. This is the fastest way for young persons to become willing to go for treatment.

Parents need to be kind but firm in refusing to pick up the pieces when their child gets in trouble. Most addicts are not open to treatment until they get to the end of their rope. This "nowhere else to turn" state of mind may come through loss of a job, the fear of losing one's spouse, children, or another valued personal relationship.

Prevention

Better than treating for drug or alcohol abuse is preventing it. You have been and continue to be a model to your adult child in your own attitudes toward drugs of all kinds. Both of us strongly urge parents to abstain from alcohol use. This is the best model for our children and also the surest protection from becoming addicted ourselves. There are currently 12 million alcoholics in the United States, but, according to the National Institute on Alcohol Abuse and Alcoholism, more than half of all Americans have a close family member who has abused alcohol or is addicted.[3] It is true that some young adults who grew up in homes where parents were abstainers became alcoholics and drug addicts, but their numbers are minuscule compared to those who grew up in homes where parents modeled social drinking. We need a radical shift in our thinking and living if we are going to turn the tide against the devastating results of alcohol and drug abuse in our society.

The most effective way to keep your adolescent children from getting involved in drugs and alcohol is to love them unconditionally, speaking love in a language that communicates to them emotionally, and keeping their love tanks full; and also modeling for them a life of abstinence from drugs and alcohol. In so doing you can demonstrate to them that one can experience life to the fullest without reliance on external chemical influence. Many parents may disagree, but we deeply believe abstinence is the best policy, sending a consistent signal to our children. Our views are based on personal experience and on our many years of helping people, Ross as a family psychiatrist and Gary as a pastor and counselor.

If your child is already using drugs and/or alcohol but is not addicted, be sure you give unconditional love and also educational information about the dangers of consumption. If, however, your child is already addicted to drugs or alcohol, the only lasting solution is to get him or her into a treatment program. This means you will need to do your homework about the various kinds of programs as well as their cost.

ATTENTION-DEFICIT (HYPERACTIVE) DISORDER

The fourth hurdle to becoming a mature adult is attention deficit (hyperactive) disorder, an ongoing syndrome affecting between 3 and 5 percent of all children. In almost two-thirds of children with ADHD, symptoms persist to varying degrees into adulthood. These disturbances disrupt vital areas, such as attention, ability to think, impulse control, memory, body control, and coordination. Children with ADHD are prone to having other problems in adult life. Eighty-five percent of adults with ADHD are found to have various psychological conditions such as anxiety, depression, unstable moods, personality problems, and alcohol or substance abuse problems.[4] It is consequently more difficult to treat these people, because the underlying ADHD is seldom recognized and goes untreated.

If you suspect that your adult child is afflicted with ADHD, we encourage you to read books and articles by reputable professionals in the field. There is much controversy surrounding ADHD and much erroneous material is being written.

The treatment of ADHD in adults, as well as children, must be tailored to the individual, because each person responds differently. Although certainly not the only treatment for ADHD in adults, medication is frequently the most effective. At least 60 percent of adult patients experience a substantial and often dramatic response to medications. When their symptoms lessen, they are more amenable to the treatment of other problems. The overall benefits of a combined and successful treatment may very well prove to be of life-changing proportions. Paul Wender, MD, summarizing research findings, reports improvements in seven different areas including hyperactivity, where "fidgeting and restlessness decrease"; inattention, where "concentration is enhanced, and distractability diminished or disappears"; and temper, where "the threshold for anger is raised and patients become less irascible."[5]

Because finding the right treatment for ADHD can be difficult, we recommend calling your local medical society as a way of beginning to find the best help in your area.

A FINAL HURDLE: CONSUMERISM

One other hurdle trips up many adult children on their journey to independence. Unlike the first four hurdles, it creates little physical or psychological consequences, though it contributes to much stress and limits their future. The hurdle is *consumerism*, and to many young adults it seems both fun and unthreatening.

"Buy Things and Have Fun"

Many in Generation Y and X have been drawn to a materialistic lifestyle, particularly in the affluence of recent years prior to the current economic slump. They want money to buy things and to have fun. From high-end jeans to frequent dining out to the latest offerings from Apple, our young adults are using credit cards and big loans to gain lots of goods. They are caught in consumerism.

To be fair, some of us boomer parents have chased this materialistic dream too, and we have passed it on to our offspring. We regret what we taught, but now our adult children mimic us.

We older adults, and many baby boomers, lived our early years at a time when there was no opportunity to live well without having a steady job, working hard, and saving our money. When we were able, we wanted to give our children all the advantages we could afford and so we took them hiking, skiing, traveling. Those who want to continue with these activities may not even try to live within their means—and credit cards make this possible. Their desire for fun keeps many young people in financial straits. Consumerism hinders an adult child's independence in many ways. Indeed, worries and stress over debt have become battlefields in many young adult marriages. Failure to discuss debt with a prospective marriage partner can set up the marriage for deceit and ultimate failure.

When possessions become more important than people, relationships inevitably suffer. Meanwhile, single adults often find themselves so far in debt that they see no way out; such an attitude fosters depression.

The false idea that one "can have it all" reflects immature thinking. The reality is we cannot have everything we want. Delayed gratification is one of the signs of maturity. Yet consumerism has become bondage for many young adults.

Model Responsibility

Parents can help their children escape consumerism several ways. The first begins when the children are young. Brace yourself to use the word *no*, even when it is difficult. Start when they are still living at home, or you may discover that you have become a teacher of financial irresponsibility. Many young couples today face marriage with very high debt levels, part of it for their education but another large part for purchases on credit. They have no realistic plan for paying off their debts, which can reach $30,000 or more between them.

Second, don't automatically bail out your adult children. When they face their dilemma, some young adults call on their parents for financial aid. If you have done this in the past, it is not too late to change your ways. You can admit to your child, "I realize that I have failed in my efforts to help you learn how to handle finances. I had plenty and wanted to share with you, but I've done it in a way that has made you dependent on me. That is not a good position for you. I know that you want to be self-sufficient and I apologize that I haven't helped you reach that goal earlier. I want us to rethink what we are doing and find a way for you to learn how to live on a budget that is within your grasp. What are your thoughts about this?"

Whether we realize it or not, most of us have deep feelings about helping an adult child financially. Some of us feel adamantly that everyone should be able to "make it on his own" and that it is immature to seek help from parents. Others, usually without realizing it, are so anxious for their offspring that they find it hard to say no. Either extreme can be harmful; there are appropriate times and situations for helping an adult child, but we must take care in how and when we do so.

When your child requests financial assistance, you should not rush to conclusions but listen to the whole story. Depending on the situation, it may be appropriate and loving to help financially. Ask questions to make sure you understand the request and also to assure your child that you care. If you jump to a decision, or sound as if you have, you run the risk of making a mistake and also hurting your child. In most decisions about money, it is wise to delay, giving yourself time to think it over. It takes time to think, and even more time to discuss the matter with your spouse. Both parents must feel good about the decision that is made. This is another occasion to pray about the matter, for wisdom and a sense of peace.

After you have given the request sufficient thought and prayer, you can give a reasonable reply to your child. If your answer is not what your adult child wanted, you need to make sure that you do not argue with the child about your decision. You'll want to be understanding, pleasant, and firm, and also avoid being manipulated. Give your answer, your reasons, and then move on to something else. If appropriate, you can consider advising your child on other possible ways to meet the need.

When You Decide to Help

If you decide that you want to lend or give your child some money, be careful in the way you manage the loan or gift, so that the real need is met and the financial situation of you and your spouse and also of the young person is not put in jeopardy. Even with a child, it is usually well to have the terms of a loan agreement on paper and a signature affixed.

Most financial advisers warn against lending large amounts of money to adult children, especially young adult children. Most such loans would never be made by banks because the young adult cannot demonstrate the ability and has limited resources to repay the loan. When parents grant such a loan, they put the young adult child in a no-win situation. The child probably will be unable to repay the loan and, when the nonpayment occurs, it inevitably creates ill will between parents and the child.

Many young people ask favors instead of money—favors that give them a monetary advantage. The most common are in the area of child care or work on their home. You need to be fully comfortable with what you agree to do for them. Otherwise, resentment will build on your part and the requests will continue on theirs.

In all your dealings with your children about finances and/or favors, keep in mind that you should do nothing that will threaten your long-term relationship. You don't want a conflict now to harm the quality of family life now or for the future. Remember, the goal is always to bring your adult children to independence and maturity.

CONFLICTS over lifestyle ISSUES

I n the fifties it was called "shacking up." Today it's "cohabitation," or more simply, "living together." In the fifties it was called "homosexuality"; now it's "gay lifestyle," or "sexual preference." In the fifties the child out of wedlock was "illegitimate"; now the newborn is a "love child," the outcome of what one U.S. governmental agency politely calls "nonmarital childbearing."

The new names reflect more than a change of vocabulary. They signal new, often value-free attitudes toward life.

Our adult children—and, in fact, most Americans born after about 1965—have been influenced by a moral milieu that has said anything goes. They have been part of a sexual revolution of choice; watchers of TV messages that began to dominate homes and offer value-free programming; consumers of a wide-open Internet. Thus many Generation Xers and Millennials grew up assuming that alternate lifestyles were acceptable. Many believe that right and wrong are relative. For them, morality is not the issue. Instead they value the freedom to choose their own lifestyle in every part of life. For them, the only absolute is that there are no moral absolutes.

If you have different values, traditional values that reflect the Judeo-Christian ethic, you may chafe at the lifestyle practiced or advocated by your at-home adult child. Even if you are among those boomer parents who engaged in youthful experimentation yourself, you may feel uneasy when you see your children behaving in ways you never did. When it's *your* kids, it's different. It seems that something has gone awry, but you don't know how to deal with it.

Whether you continue to believe in moral absolutes or simply prefer that your children not engage in behavior that makes you uncomfortable, you probably are disturbed when you watch your children follow the morally ambiguous road. When adult children visit or live in their parents' homes, conflict over moral standards and lifestyle choices is almost inevitable. As a parent, you may feel intense emotional pain, disrespect, or even rejection when the choices of your adult children violate traditional standards of behavior and thought.

In this chapter, we will discuss a couple of the more common alternative lifestyles that have created conflicts between parents and their young adult children. The most obvious of these is the area of sexuality, which we will treat in two sections. The other is religious choices.

HOMOSEXUALITY

Almost all parents—even those who say they will tolerate all lifestyles—will feel shock and deep hurt if one of their children announces he is homosexual.[1] An initial reaction is that they have failed their child in some crucial way. For this reason, many adult children don't immediately or ever announce their involvement in this lifestyle.

Most parents expect their children to be heterosexual and most are devastated if their children reveal a strong sexual desire for the same sex. As a parent, be aware that in most cases if one has a strong homosexual desire, the attraction to members of the same sex will continue even if the individual chooses a heterosexual or celibate lifestyle. Because this is so, parents must deal with the problem and come to some resolution.

Distinguish Orientation from Lifestyle

Significantly, parents must distinguish between a homosexual orientation and a homosexual lifestyle. Orientation has to do with inner emotional, sexual desires, whereas lifestyle has to do with overt sexual behavior. Though a son or daughter is attracted to members of the same sex, he or she is not compelled to live a homosexual lifestyle. The child can show self-control and abstinence, even as an unmarried heterosexual adult can before marriage. In the Judeo-Christian tradition, as in all other major world religions, the homosexual lifestyle is viewed as abnormal and sinful. Yet, the literature from these traditions acknowledges the existence of people with a homosexual orientation, as well as persons with various other sexual attractions: bestiality, pedophilia, transvestitism, etc. These desires are viewed as temptations to pervert the divinely ordained purposes of human sexuality. The moral challenge is to resist such temptation. Most of these religious traditions also call upon the heterosexual to control sexual desires. This involves abstinence for significant periods of one's life, and for some a lifetime of chastity.

Most religious traditions are sympathetic with the person who has a homosexual orientation, but they do not view a homosexual lifestyle as acceptable sexual behavior. There is acceptance of the person but rejection of the behavior. There is even redemption. Indeed, Paul the apostle wrote about former sexual practitioners, including "adulterers" and "homosexuals," that "you were washed, you were sanctified, you were justified in the name of the Lord Jesus Christ."[2] Various religious organizations, such as Exodus International, have focused on a sympathetic ministry to homosexuals, helping those who choose to discover freedom from the homosexual lifestyle. Many go on to establish heterosexual marriages, while others live a life of chastity.

Modern research has failed to discover the causes of a homosexual orientation. No one has proved a genetic cause of homosexual practice or shown homosexuality is an inherent, biological urge.[3] No one knows why one child from a household turns out to be homosexual while the others are heterosexual. The authors are increasingly aware of the deep turmoil the young person feels when he realizes that he is different from the norm. The rejection from friends is heightened when his parents also spurn him. If he is part of a religious family, his pain can seem unbearable; he knows that his orientation is condemned. It may help religious parents empathize if they can realize that whether the homosexual child wants to change or not, he is still a person, their flesh and blood, created by God with inherent value and needing support as he finds his identity.

There continues to be much controversy, even among experts, on the treatment of homosexuality. But regardless of how parents categorize homosexuality—as unnatural, abnormal, and even sinful—it is present in a certain number of persons and needs to be dealt with in a redemptive manner. We want to offer suggestions that may be helpful to you.

Accept Your Child

All parents who are having difficulty relating to their adult children who have chosen a homosexual lifestyle should remember the central message of the Christian faith. The Scriptures declare loudly that "all have sinned."[4] We are not in a position to condemn our children for what we believe to be wrong or sinful behavior. Remember the words of Jesus when the crowds were ready to stone the woman who was caught in the act of adultery: "If any one of you is without sin, let him be the first to throw a stone at her."[5] The Christian message is that we all are sinners equally fallen before a holy God who reached out to us by sending Christ to deliver us from sins.[6] Thus, we are to love all who stray, including our children, just as God loves us. Jesus was criticized by the religious people of His day because He associated with sinners, but He knew that He could not influence people without being with them. We too will have our greatest influence if we accept our children, spend time with them, communicate with them, and demonstrate our love for them, even though we do not approve of their lifestyle.

When I, Ross, opened a Christian mental health unit in a local hospital, I conferred with the clinical director, a fine Christian man whom I'll call Howard. As we were planning the program, Howard said that we should not allow homosexuals on the unit. At first, I thought he meant that we should make sure none of the staff was homosexual. I was shocked when he said that we should refuse treatment.

"But Howard, we have a moral and ethical commitment to serve everyone, regardless of sexual orientation."

He shook his head. "No, I believe a Christian unit should not treat homosexuals. Homosexuality is condemned in Scripture as sinful, and we should have nothing to do with it."

I tried to explain that Christ died for everyone, not just certain people. "Part of our reason for having a Christian unit was to witness and share our faith with everyone," I said. "Jesus came to earth because He loved the world and wanted to redeem it, not condemn it."

I never did convince my clinical director. Howard and others did finally agree that we had no choice, however, when I told them that it was against the law to refuse medical service to anyone in need.

Parents need to look beyond the sexual orientation and love the person. If we do not, we estrange them in our homes and our hearts. A Christian approach to homosexuals or lesbians will be redemptive, not condemning. As physician Del DeHart notes, those with strong homosexual desires "may be our friends, our acquaintances, or our children. If our rhetoric wrongly convinces them that they are uniquely evil because of the desires they have, many will leave the church and embrace the radical gay community for acceptance. Others will simply live a bitter lie for fear of receiving rejection rather than loving support."[7]

You certainly have nothing to gain by rejecting your adult child if he or she is a practicing homosexual. You have much to gain if you continue to respect, love, and demonstrate that love to your child. This does not mean accepting a gay or lesbian lifestyle, nor does it mean enduring behavior that puts undue stress on you. You should be courteous to your child's friend, but you do not need to allow the other person to spend the night at your home in the same bedroom. It usually boils down to common sense.

As long as you are loving, kind, and as helpful as you can reasonably be, you are on the right track to gradually finding ways of having a more positive influence on the one you have raised. As time passes, your own feelings will be more stable as will your relationship with your child. Parents who reject their children, however, create unbelievable pain and often a permanent separation.

Find Help for Yourself

Your situation will indicate the type of help you need. Therapy is often helpful to parents who are dealing with their responses to discovering they have a homosexual child, including feelings of confusion, depression, shock, and anxiety. Talking with a competent counselor can help you sort out those feelings, regain perspective, and learn how best to deal with the situation.

Support groups are particularly beneficial to parents of lesbian and homosexual children. As parents express their attitudes during the meetings, those attitudes and feelings can be dealt with in healthy and compassionate ways. Parents will discover that other fine people are experiencing the same pain, and they can share their ways of coping with the problems.

HETEROSEXUAL COHABITATION

Living Together: A Growing Trend

Cohabitation is fast becoming an acceptable lifestyle for couples of all ages. Now unmarried men and women live in the same house for months, even years, before getting married—if they marry at all. About half of all children born in this country are now born to unmarried couples. Many young people believe living together without benefit of marriage is a totally justified way of forming life's most intimate relationship. Permissive influences in society and fear of commitment are the main reasons they cohabit. They find their choice glorified in the media and taken for granted by many of their peers. So they share meals, money, and the same bed.

Heterosexual cohabiting means living in the same dwelling in order to enjoy the pleasures of marriage, especially sexual relations, without the responsibility of marriage. While many do this openly, some may maintain separate dwellings for the sake of their families or appearances. Thus your adult child may live with you but spend nights at the friend's house (or invite the friend to spend nights at your house). One unspoken reason for cohabitation may be to upset the authority figures in their lives. When this is the case, one or both parties of the couple is exhibiting passive-aggressive behavior—the most harmful expression of anger.

Rules of the House

If your adult child lives at home, be sure to have house rules concerning overnight guests. Your child may want his girlfriend (or her boyfriend) to stay in the same room but in "separate beds" or to "use my bed, and I'll sleep on the floor." Is that realistic? Probably not, so determine those house rules ahead of time. If the adult child has an apartment but stays overnight for several days (on weekends or holidays, for instance) and wants to bring his friend, again establish house rules. His relationship does not mean you must tolerate inappropriate sexual acting out in your home. Remaining pleasant and firm, you may require that your adult child and the friend sleep in separate bedrooms if they choose to spend the night in your home.

Our attitudes as parents are important. If we are upset, belligerent, or scold our children who have live-in arrangements, they will likely display an even more tenacious defiance. It is usually better for parents to express their beliefs in tones as gentle as possible and then leave it. Saying more will strengthen the passive-aggressive resistance. Parents need to remember that the only chance they have for influencing their children is through the relationship that already exists between the parent and the adult child.

What Should Parents Do?

So, what are parents to do when they find themselves in conflict with their child's sexual behavior? Some parents have tried the ostrich approach, denying that it is happening. There is little to be gained from this approach except perhaps momentary peace of mind. Sooner or later, the reality will be unavoidable. Other parents use the missile approach—taking every opportunity to shoot verbal missiles at the young people, to condemn their behavior. Such reaction damages parental influence now and in the future.

It can be difficult for parents caught in this situation to be civil to a child's partner, and yet to be unpleasant is a serious mistake that can drive the child into a deeper commitment. Also, if your child ends up marrying the person, your future relationship with the young family is damaged. It is usually better to treat your child's live-in mate as a likable person and show common courtesies to him or her. We realize this may be extremely difficult for you, but with God's grace you can behave with love and kindness, even though you do not approve of their behavior. You can still appreciate the person while not approving the behavior. Your tone of voice, a handshake greeting, and occasional hugs all can help maintain an amicable relationship with the child and his or her friend. At the same time, you may give cautions and ask questions of your child about the relationship to show your concern and dissatisfaction with the live-in situation.

It is important that you have the support of family and friends; you may even need counseling to be able to maintain an even attitude and behavior toward the young people. Also, you should remind yourself that your child loves you and needs you, and that he knows exactly how you are affected by his behavior. He knows that your continuing to be a loving parent does not mean that you approve of what he is doing or that you are violating your own values.

Just as you have sought to give your child unconditional love in the past, regardless of behavior, so also you will do the same now. You want to be a positive influence on your child in the future, and this means that you cannot afford to break the relationship you have.

Seeking an Open Dialogue

With the abandonment of moral absolutes, many young adults have also jettisoned the concept of parental authority. Their attitude seems to be, "Why should we listen to you?" If we are to have a positive influence on them, whether it be about a cohabitation arrangement or homosexuality, we must seek to relate to them as persons. That includes being willing to listen to their ideas, consider their points of view, and affirm their logic and perspectives where we can. Therefore the authors advocate an open dialogue. Honestly disagree where you must; ask probing questions without feeling that you need to answer your own questions. Expose your children to the results of modern social research on the consequences of certain sexual lifestyles but let them wrestle with the realities of the research;[8] and don't preach.

This does not mean that you should not share your pain at what you believe to be wrong choices. It does mean that you will not use that pain as a tool of manipulation. We can offer noncondemning statements that we hope will create a climate where the young adults can receive and even request our advice. It is crucial that we recognize their autonomy and give them freedom to make their own choices, even when we disagree with them.

Give your children freedom to make their own decisions. They may well suffer the consequences of those choices. If they do begin to reap negative consequences of what we believe are poor decisions in their sexual behavior, we dare not limit or actively remove those consequences of their behavior. Of course, we can certainly walk with them through those painful consequences. That's part of being redemptive. It is in this context that many parents build deep and abiding relationships with their broken and suffering young adults. Our emotional support may be what they need to help them make corrections in this part of life.

Showing Your Love: The Moores

Being pleasant, keeping communication open, and continuing to show love are all ways to respond to a cohabitation situation. Jerome and Felicia Moore displayed those qualities to all three daughters, but they learned to continue to extend it when the oldest disappointed them with a cohabiting relationship. Lisa had been a "perfect" child growing up. An excellent student and good athlete, attractive and with many friends, she was a joy to all who knew her. She was close to her sisters and also was active in her church. Lisa did well in her college studies and graduated with honors. Then she took a job in a nearby town and was progressing in her chosen field of work.

After she had settled in her new apartment, she asked her parents to come for a visit. When Jerome and Felicia arrived, they experienced "the shock of our lives" as they saw that Lisa was living with Michael, the young man the parents had met during her college years. The two young people had talked about the possibility of marriage during their years in school and decided to find jobs in the same area so that they could continue their relationship. As they discussed it further, they decided they were not ready for marriage but that they would like to try living together.

Fortunately, Jerome and Felicia were able to handle themselves maturely. They listened to the young couple in bewilderment and realized that Lisa and Michael knew all too well what their feelings were. They could even see that the young couple had carefully planned their presentation and were ready for the parents' reactions.

Felicia and Jerome gently asked the young couple appropriate questions and made known their concerns and wishes clearly and lovingly, but without being unpleasant, even though their hearts were breaking. After they left for home, they cried together, but decided that maintaining their relationship with Lisa and Michael was the most critical factor for them.

Much to their delight, the Moores were often invited to spend time with Lisa and Michael. Over time they realized that Michael was an exceptionally fine young man, the type of person they would have chosen for Lisa. The Moores just wished the two would marry. Both Felicia and Jerome had a deep Christian faith, and they prayed fervently about the situation and asked friends to pray with them. Jerome was so concerned that he went on a prayer and fasting vigil for three days.

One day Michael and Lisa invited the parents to dinner at the apartment. Over dessert the young couple asked their advice about plans for marriage. They revealed that the parents' kindness and love to the couple had much to do with the decision to follow the Moores' wishes and example. That night Jerome and Felicia returned home, thanking God for answers to their prayers. They also were profoundly grateful that as parents they had said or done nothing that would have alienated their daughter.

If you have a situation similar to this one and you have handled it well, but it has not turned out as wonderfully, don't despair. Don't second-guess yourself and wonder if you should have been more forceful, confronting, demanding. Or, if you have been inappropriately overbearing, demanding, or otherwise unpleasant, you can always apologize and start on a better road with your loved one. And we believe prayer can prepare your heart, giving you sensitivity, wisdom, and peace.[9]

RELIGIOUS CHOICES
A Source of Great Pain

Another area in which young adults can provoke frustration in their parents is religion. Because religious beliefs are often tied strongly to our emotions, when adult children make religious choices that differ from parents, we can feel great pain.

Our children's changing religious beliefs can express themselves in many ways. Besides choosing a different church or synagogue, adult children may choose not to attend church or the synagogue (or mosque) at all. They may marry someone of a different faith or decide not to send their own children to church, feeling that "the children should be free to choose." These adult children may also join religious groups that the parents consider to be "cultic" and dangerous. Such decisions can make us parents feel like failures. The decisions also can spark fear that the children are making a mistake that will have lasting consequences.

In addition, all religions include not only a core set of beliefs by which people try to live but numerous traditions that affect all of life. Our religious beliefs influence how we conduct weddings and funerals; they affect what holidays we celebrate and how we celebrate them. The importance of Bar Mitzvah, baptism, and the sacraments depends upon one's religion. Perhaps most important, our religion largely influences our values. Our religion affects what we see as right and wrong, how we view life after death, and what one must do in this life to fare well in the next.

All these influences affect our—and our children's—sense of identity and heritage. When one of our adult children changes or ignores his religion, often it sparks tension between us. "What! You're not going to get married in the church?"

The number one question in the minds of parents experiencing religious conflict with their children is: "What shall I do now?" There are only two basic choices: 1. Abandon them; reject them because you disagree with their choice. 2. Relate to them; keep the doors of communication open.

We believe the wise parent will choose number two. Learn to process your own frustration and learn to talk with—and listen to—your child in a noncontrolling manner.

A Different Religion . . . a Different Church

Maria was Jewish, but she was not a happy mother. Her daughter Stella had been attending a Christian church while in college. At first Maria thought, *It's okay. Stella is a good girl. She is in college and exploring other beliefs, but she has strong roots. She will keep her Jewish faith.* But Maria was hurt, then angry, and finally livid when Stella told her that she had accepted Jesus as her Messiah and had been baptized in the Christian church.

"What about your family? Don't you care about us? You have betrayed us! What about your wedding? What about your children? What about your future?

"Oh Stella, we must talk to the rabbi. We have a serious problem."

Maria's pain is real, and it is deep. The pain will not be easily resolved. Many Jewish, Christian, Muslim, Hindu, Buddhist, and other religious mothers can identify with Maria. For many parents, their greatest fear is that their children will abandon the faith of their parents.

Richard was forced to deal with this issue of how to respond when his two children were still in high school and chose to change Protestant denominations. Sean and Brittany had grown up in the Episcopal church where their family had been involved for five generations. Now, they decided that they wanted to go to a nearby Baptist church where the worship was, they said, more "vibrant" and the youth program one that was popular with many of their friends. At first Richard hoped it was an experiment that would be short-lived. When they insisted, "This is the church of our choice and we want to become members," Richard was angry. He wanted to ask them, "What will your grandparents think? How can you walk away from such a long-standing tradition in our family?" but he said nothing. Instead, he tried to calmly reason with Sean and Brittany, an approach that got him nowhere.

Next, he offered to double their allowance and even pay for Baptist summer camp if they would just stay in the family's church. Their reply was, "We don't want to go to the Episcopal church." Then Richard tried threats. Nothing changed their minds. As a last resort, Richard shared his plight with his rector, who asked, "Richard, did you ever want to go to another church when you were growing up?"

"Yes, and I did several times during college."

"And why did you return to the Episcopal church?"

"Well, it seemed more like home. It just seemed the right thing to do."

"But it was your choice?" his rector pried. "Your parents didn't force you to return?"

"No. I knew it was what they desired, but they certainly didn't force me."

"Then, isn't that what you wish for Sean and Brittany? That they will choose the Episcopal church of their own free will, not because you forced them to come?"

"Well, yes," said Richard, "but they're still in high school."

"Rather than fighting their choices, why don't you try giving them freedom? You might even visit the Baptist church with them so you can intelligently discuss some of the ideas to which they are being exposed."

Richard left the office feeling that the whole world had ganged up on him, including his own minister. Yet, on reflection, he knew the rector was right. He went home and told his children, "I've been thinking about this church thing and I've decided that I must give you the freedom to make your own decision. I'm sorry for the way I've tried to manipulate and control you. And, I apologize for the harsh things I've said about the Baptist church. I realize that this is a choice the two of you must make, and I want you to have that freedom. In fact, some Sunday soon I want to go to church with you. To be honest, I've been in a Baptist church only once, and I'd like to learn more about it."

"Great," said Sean. "Any Sunday. Let us know."

Brittany hugged her dad and Sean shook his hand, and Richard was now back in a position to exert a positive influence on his children's religious decisions.

Cults and "Toxic" Religions

For many young adults, the opportunities for religious experimentation greatly expand when they leave home for college or work. Numerous religious voices are calling on the college campus and beyond. Young people who respond to these voices often are from homes that are nominally religious but with very low involvement. This lack of moral and spiritual guidance has created a vacuum in their hearts and they are open to listening to religious voices from different backgrounds. They are looking for something in which they can believe and for a group to which they can belong.

Impelled by their own inner longings to find ultimate meaning in life, many of them become involved in groups whose beliefs and practices are far removed from those of their families and communities. Some of these groups have been dubbed by researchers as "toxic religions" because of the strong controlling nature of those who lead them and also because of the loss of personal autonomy experienced by members. When parents learn of their children's involvement with such groups, they are usually appalled to discover that they are already deeply entrenched in bizarre beliefs and practices. Parental responses vary widely. On one extreme are those who, with the help of paid deprogrammers, arrange for elaborate rescue schemes to kidnap their children from the groups. These efforts are seldom ultimately productive because they create more animosity. When the young people are free, they usually return to their friends or get involved in another religious group of their choice.

We believe it is far healthier for parents to seek to maintain lines of communication with their children. We are fully aware that some cultic groups go to great lengths to prohibit members from having contact with their families, and this tactic alone is a warning that the group is indeed toxic. Any religion that refuses freedom of choice ceases to be religious in the highest sense, because it has in reality become a prison. Parents should not allow the rules of such a cultic group to keep them from trying to make contact with their children. Letters, phone calls, email, or any other form of communication should be explored as a means to keep in touch.

When it is possible, parents will want to visit their children and sit in on some of the religious sessions. If this is not possible, they can seek to learn about the group from research or from those who live near the community. Whatever contact parents are able to make should be friendly and noncombative. Any positive gesture or gift leaves the young adult with a pleasant experience and a physical token that has a tie to home and childhood. If the young person can leave for a visit at home, the door is open for conversation in a more neutral setting. Such exchange of ideas should be honest but noncondemning. Parents need to distinguish between disagreeing with the beliefs of children and condemning them for holding those beliefs. Some parents fear that if they admit to giving their children freedom to hold their own beliefs, they are encouraging them to pursue belief systems that they consider harmful. Actually, the opposite is true. Religious and spiritual beliefs and practices must be left to the young adult. Parents can have an influence at that point but cannot control.

A Global Village

Increasingly we are a global village, and our adult children are being exposed to different religions in the community, at school, and through the media. Their own beliefs are being challenged and shaped by these religions. Thus a Muslim can go to college and find himself seated next to a Buddhist, with a Christian in front of him and an atheist beside him. Brad found himself in a similar situation, having his beliefs challenged by a follower of another religion. As a college freshman his roommate was a Hindu from India. Brad grew up in a nominal Christian home and considered himself Christian, but he liked his new friend and they did many things together. He became fascinated with the Hindu respect for life, and in a world religions class he wrote a paper on Hinduism. In his research, he read much of Hindu philosophy and lifestyle. By the end of the school year, Brad announced to his parents that he had decided to become a Hindu. His parents were horrified. They did not know much about Hinduism, but they remembered a movie they saw years ago in which the Hindu wife was burned alive with her dead husband so that they could be together in the afterlife.

Fortunately, Brad's parents went to their minister before they overreacted. The minister wisely advised them to express interest in Brad's new religion, rather than condemning him for his choice. He reminded them, "College is the time when many young adults explore other world religions. They are developing their own self-identity, and religion is one area in which this emerging independence is evidenced."

If parents are harsh, condemning, and rigid, they lose the opportunity to influence their child's future thinking. The young person sees his parents as "out of touch" and refuses to discuss religious matters with them. If parents can be accepting of their child's freedom to explore other religions and will openly discuss the merits of other belief systems, they will also have the opportunity to share what they perceive to be the inconsistencies or detrimental practices of these religions. Open but noncondemning dialogue offers the potential to further influence the young person's thinking. However, angry, explosive statements of condemnation shut down the possibility of further communication.

As a parent, you may be deeply troubled with your child's religious interest. However, you must not forfeit your future influence or relationship by dogmatically condemning your child for having such interests. A young adult is in the process of developing his or her own religious beliefs. It will help you to realize that this is a normal part of the developmental transition to adulthood. Children may express interest in several world religions before settling into their own belief system. If you can walk with them through this process, by reading about these religions and talking openly with your children, you can be an influential part of this process. But, if you condemn the pursuit, your children must walk alone or choose other mentors.

Honest and Vulnerable Sharing

The greatest influence you as parents have on your children's religious beliefs happens in the first eighteen years of their lives, as the children listen to what you say and observe what you do. The closer your practice is to your preaching, the more respect they have for you and your beliefs. But, the greater the distance between what you proclaim and what you practice, the less likely they are to follow your religious beliefs.

This does not mean that your religious influence ends when they become adults. For those who recognize past failures, it is never too late to say, "I realize that when you were growing up, my lifestyle did not demonstrate very well what I claimed to believe. In more recent days, I've changed my thinking and behavior in many areas and wish I could go back and live parts of my life again. Of course, that's impossible, but I want you to know that I regret the way I failed you. I hope we will have opportunity to share with each other something of our personal beliefs and practices in the future." Such honest and vulnerable sharing of your heart has the potential of creating a fresh climate of openness between the two of you.

becoming an
IN-LAW and a
GRANDPARENT

Just after Jake completed his MBA from a prestigious university, he married Jenny. The two had dated for several years, fallen in love, and looked forward to becoming husband and wife. While Jake was studying for his master's degree, Jenny had lived at home with her parents and worked as an accountant with a local firm. Just before graduation Jake secured a job with a company whose headquarters were in his hometown. His job would start when they returned from their honeymoon.

The couple found and furnished an apartment and anticipated that their first year of marriage would be the happiest of their lives. Unfortunately, it turned out to be the most painful.

Their conflicts centered around Jenny's parents. To put it in Jake's words, "She is married to them. I'm just a boyfriend. If it's convenient to be with me, fine; but her parents come first."

Jenny insisted that this was not true. "Jake is number one in my life, but I also want a good relationship with my parents. I don't think I should have to choose between them." She did acknowledge that there had been times when she and Jake had plans; then her parents would call and she would change their plans to accommodate them. This infuriated Jake.

Jake's parents, Jim and Betsy, learned of the difficulties during a telephone call from Jake. "Mom, I know we invited you folks out for dinner tonight, but this afternoon, Jenny got a call from her mother asking if we could come over and stay with her brother who is sick. Her parents have a business engagement and don't want to leave David alone. Jenny told them we would come before discussing it with me.

"I'm not very happy about this," Jake added. "David is definitely old enough to stay by himself for a few hours, but Jenny feels that we'd be letting her parents down if we didn't go. I hope you guys understand."

"Of course, Jake," his mother answered. "That's fine. We can go out another time." As she tried to be reassuring, she could tell by Jake's tone of voice that this was a bigger problem than simply taking care of Jenny's sick brother. Her apprehensions were realized a month later when Jake was sitting at her table.

"Mom, I don't know how to tell you this, but Jenny and I have serious problems. Her parents are so demanding and she doesn't know how to stand up to them. Whatever they ask, she feels she must do. They're trying to control us and I can't take it. They are so different from Dad and you. I had no idea that they were so demanding or that they would require so much of Jenny's time. Her mother treats her as though she was still living at home and we weren't even married. She acts hurt if Jenny doesn't go shopping with her every time she calls. She is very manipulating and tries to make Jenny feel it's practically a sin if she doesn't do everything her mother wants. I thought Jenny was stronger than that, but I guess I was wrong. I've talked with her, but she doesn't hear what I'm saying. She thinks I want her to abandon her folks. That's not it at all. I just want her to be my wife first and their daughter second."

BETSY'S RESPONSE

Now, what would you do if your adult child had a marital problem and shared his heart? How would you get involved—if at all? For Betsy, she wanted first to take Jake in her arms and tell him that everything was going to be all right. She wanted to kiss his knee, like she did when he was eight, and assure him that the pain would go away. But he wasn't eight anymore and this pain wasn't a skinned knee. She knew that she couldn't solve his marital problems, but she did have a perspective she decided to share with him.

"Jake, I appreciate your telling me this. I know it is serious and is causing you a lot of pain. I also know that in the first year of marriage, many couples have similar problems. Those who make it deal with their problems in a realistic way. The couples who don't make it are the ones who sweep their problems under the rug, trying to act as if they don't exist. In reality, the problems just get larger.

"Sharing this with me is a first step. Now I want to encourage you to take a second. I'm not the one to give you marriage counseling, but that's what you and Jenny need. There is a counselor on our church staff; and I also know two good ones downtown. If money is a problem, Dad and I can help. The important thing is that both of you talk to someone with skills in helping couples work through such difficulties. Don't let it go on or it will just get worse."

Jake replied, "I don't know if she'll go. She'd be really upset if she knew I was talking to you about this."

"Then perhaps you can tell her that you are going for counseling because you need help in dealing with your own struggle," his mother answered, "and that you would like her to go with you. She may go because she wants the counselor to hear her side of the story. But, if she doesn't, you go alone. At least you will get the process started and she may join you later. Your problem isn't going to go away by itself, and you need someone to help you work through it."

Jake agreed, and when he drove home, he felt better than when he came. At least he knew the first step to take.

Jenny was reluctant, but she did go with Jake to the counselor, and in the months that followed they both learned a great deal about how to meet each other's needs and build an authentic marriage. Not only did Jenny have an unhealthy relationship with her parents, especially her mother, but Jake was obsessed with being a success in his business. During the counseling he realized he was failing to meet Jenny's emotional need for love. She desired quality time with him, but his job was so demanding that she often spent her evenings alone. She had finally decided that she might as well be with her mother as to stay home by herself.

During months of counseling, they came to understand each other better and made some significant changes. Jenny began to respond differently to her parents' requests, particularly when she and Jake had already made plans. Jake learned how to meet Jenny's need for love and to make more time for her. They have now been married five years and have a mutually fulfilling relationship.

A NEW TITLE, A NEW RELATIONSHIP

When your child marries, the relationship you have had is bound to change, as you move to embrace his or her spouse. These extended connections can bring you great happiness, or they can rain on your parade. The outcome is partly determined by your response to them.

After your child decides to marry, you acquire a new title: in-law. Not only do you have a son- or daughter-in-law who directly influences your child, but you also become related to people who will indirectly influence your adult child as they continue to influence their own married child. In addition, you may soon have another title: grandparent, and you will share your grandchildren with your son- or daughter-in-law's parents. And, if your son or daughter chooses to marry someone who already has children, you become instant grandparents.

BETSY'S WISE ADVICE

Thus your response to these new relationships can bring you happiness or heartache, joy or jealousy. Jake's mother was extremely wise in her responses to Jake's complaint about Jenny. In her counsel we can find several positive principles on how we parents can respond to the marital difficulties experienced by many young adults.

First, she took the problem seriously. She didn't brush it off by saying, "Oh, it can't be that bad. You're just overreacting. Take her out to dinner and she'll be all right." She didn't say, "Why don't you just talk to Jenny about this? I'm sure if she realized what you're feeling, she would change." Nor did she suggest, "Just give her some time and be patient. I'm sure it will all work out." The fact is that marital problems don't "just work out." Our high divorce statistics are stark reminders that problems unattended get worse. As concerned parents, we should respond to signs of marital problems.

Second, she did not take sides. You can become involved without saying one spouse (usually your child) is right and the other is wrong. You don't have all the facts, and to take sides could alienate the other spouse. Note that Betsy didn't tell Jake it was his fault. Nor did she blame Jenny for giving in to her mother. Instead, she remained neutral. Seldom can the responsibility for marital conflict be laid at the feet of one partner; generally, both husband and wife have done and said things to compound the problem. Both need insight into the dynamics of their relationship and then need to learn to take corrective steps in creating a different climate in which their conflicts can be resolved. When parents take sides, they only add to the problems.

Third, she waited until Jake came to her for advice. As a parent, don't offer advice until you're asked. Be willing to give counsel, but wait until such counsel is requested. Betsy might have rushed in with suggestions after she first sensed something was wrong. However, had she offered advice then, Jake might have become defensive and then not turned to her later for help. The best guideline is to wait until your married children ask for help. At that point, they are more likely to follow your suggestions.

Fourth, she offered a course of action that was specific and doable. As parents, we can give recommendations, but we should be specific. Depending on the situation, you may recommend professional counseling, seeing a financial planner, or setting up a budget. Betsy recommended counseling; she also removed the possible hurdle of finances by offering to help. While she didn't force Jake to take action, she told him why she believed it would be wise.

Significantly, Betsy talked with her husband about her conversation with Jake. The two determined that their relationship with the young couple would continue just as it had been. No questions, no blame, no changed attitudes toward Jenny or her parents. Wise parents do not seek to solve the problems of their married children. They are there to make loving suggestions if these are asked for, but they do not impose themselves on their children's lives. They give their children space to build their own lives. They allow them the freedom to say no to invitations or requests that conflict with their plans or wishes. They relate to their children in ways that will foster their growth as individuals and as a couple.

As a parent and an in-law, your goal should be to support your child and his or her mate. Welcome your son- or daughter-in-law into the family with open arms. When asked, give advice. You'll always remain a parent; become a friend.

CONGRATULATIONS, YOU'RE A GRANDPARENT!

When your children marry, you know that you will probably become a grandparent someday. You may even yearn for it, to hold a grandchild in your arms, play games—and then say good-bye to parenting at the end of the day. If the years stretch on too long, some not-yet grandparents have been known to prod, to make clumsy jokes about babies, and otherwise express their eagerness to have the next generation in tow.

Maybe you are a grandparent and love it—or maybe you don't. Some grandparents take the attitude, "I raised my kids; they can raise theirs." Others think or say, "Don't call me Grandma—I'm not that old." In their research for *Grandparents/Grandchildren: The Vital Connection*, Arthur Kornhaber and Kenneth Woodward found to their dismay that a majority of the children they talked with did not have a close relationship with their grandparents.[1] We agree with Kornhaber and Woodward that the bond between grandparent and grandchild is very important. Grandparents need to nurture that bond. If we do not take this responsibility and privilege seriously, both we and our grandchildren are losers.

There are more grandparents today than ever before, because people are living longer and generally have better health. In the United States it is estimated that there are more than 70 million grandparents today, and their lifestyle has changed dramatically from that of grandparents forty years ago. In a past generation, grandparents tended to be "stay at home" kinds of people. Modern grandparents are found on cruise ships and attending Broadway plays. Formerly, grandparents were free baby-sitters whenever and wherever. Today's grandparents tend to set boundaries to protect their own way of life. Older grandparents were more easygoing and relaxed; modern grandparents can be busy and anxious about their own lives. Earlier grandparents retired and stayed that way. Modern grandparents tend to choose second and third careers. Grandma and Grandpa used to live in the same town, even on the same street, as their grandchildren. Today's grandparents may be half a country away. Grandpa and Grandma used to live under the same roof; today they may be long divorced, possibly with step-grandparents in the picture. Or, they may be raising their grandkids.

THE HEART OF THE EXTENDED FAMILY

Yet, for all the differences in style, some things remain the same. Traditionally we grandparents are the heart of the extended family. We are the family historians, the ones who keep the family tied to its roots and to the past. As we get older, we become more interested in those who preceded us and we can then share this with the younger members of the family.

Grandparents offer security and stability to grandchildren, and this is especially important in a time of change. We represent unconditional love, kindness, and understanding. We are nonjudgmental counselors. We can ease their sorrows and give encouragement during difficult times. We are there to encourage our children when they need us. We are a refuge when stress and tension become overwhelming. We are in the best position to be our grandchildren's own cheerleaders, to get excited about each one and lift high their self-esteem.

As grandparents, we can stand for spiritual guidance and strength. Many grandparents choose to pray for each grandchild as well as their parents. They offer comfort and good cheer and become role models of a

119

deep spiritual faith for their grandchildren. Israel's King Solomon wrote, "Children's children are a crown to the aged."[2] Yes, grandchildren are special gifts.

Because our role with them is different than with anyone else, our grandchildren regard us differently than they do anyone else. Because of this, we can employ those bonds to give them strength, courage, and faith as they grow. It is definitely our choice how we use our special powers to influence for good these wonderful grandchildren who have come into our lives.

TWO TRUTHS ABOUT GRANDKIDS

We wish all grandparents would remember these two truths about grandchildren: 1. They are *not* your children; and 2. They *are* your grandchildren.

The first truth seems obvious, and yet forgetting it can cause untold problems. Because you are not their parents, you should never overstep the right and authority of the parents. This means that you need to consult their parents before you give or loan them money, take them to events, or make extravagant plans. Similarly, talk to the parents before you give the grandchildren major advice. Your failure to respect parental authority can create extreme conflict between you and your adult children.

One common point of difference today is in the means of disciplining children. You may have resorted to spanking when your children were young. Many parents today do not want any spanking, and you will need to respect this. The reasons for this are not necessarily permissive; with heightened awareness of child abuse and also because of increased government involvement with families, many young parents are wary about how and when they correct their children. It is important that you know the goals and guidelines your children are employing as they raise their children. Discuss with them discipline if you like, but do not ignore their policies or try to change them. Respect your children's role as parents. If you and they work together to make the world of the growing children one of delight and security, you will be drawn closer in the bonds of family love.

The second truth also is quite obvious: they are your grandchildren, and you have an important, loving role to play. Yet it takes imagination and continuing time and contact to make your role work for you and your grandchildren. You have certain emotional and legal rights to these children, of course, but exercising these rights needs to be done with the greatest care, since you want to build a lifelong relationship with these special children. Just as you think of them in the warmest way, so you want them to regard you with particular affection.

Whether you live close by or at some distance, you need to remember that the children are constantly growing and changing. Be sensitive and alert to their needs; consult their parents for a better understanding of their abilities and interests, especially if you are not able to visit them regularly. You may be anticipating something wonderful that you want to do with or give to your grandchild, only to discover that the toy you so carefully selected is not right for his age, or that she is fully absorbed in another pursuit. You may have in mind a trip you want to share with a grandchild, and may need to recognize that what an adult thinks is most challenging may be far beyond a child's interests.

Something all grandparents can share is time. When you give time and attention, you are placing yourself at the child's disposal, to play, to read, to explore, and most of all to give unconditional love. This does not mean allowing the child to do everything he wishes. It does mean that you are always looking out for his best interests, that you love this child and are open in showing how you feel. You are always excused for giving the most extravagant and exuberant praise. You are among the few people who can make your grandchild glow, often with a level of silliness that you couldn't get away with anywhere else. Few relationships hold greater potential for mutual pleasure and affirmation than a loving grandparent-grandchild bond.

In sharing yourself, you are giving your grandchild your unique outlook on life, your ways, your memories, your skills and interests, and, most of all, your love. As the child grows and develops wider knowledge, this can become more significant, with longlasting influence on the child and great satisfaction to you.

LONG-DISTANCE GRANDPARENTING

You may be separated by geographical distance from your grand-children, but this doesn't need to mean an emotional distance. With all the facilities of modern communication, it is ever easier to stay in touch. We think of letters, phone calls, and email, but there are other ways grand-parents can strengthen the bond. Here are several examples of creative communication by grandparents separated by miles but seemingly next door through their regular contact:

• Eileen, a Midwestern grandma, shares books with her granddaughter in Florida. She buys two copies of the same book and sends one to Sheila. They read the same chapter each week, and on the weekend Grandma calls Sheila on the phone to talk with each other about the story—what they liked or didn't like. This can lead to interesting discussions about Sheila's feelings and sometimes about life itself. When they finish that book, Sheila buys the next set of books. We think these two will be reading buddies for life.

• Harry has recently become computer literate. Each month he com-poses a short story and sends it via email to his great-granddaughter in California. Sara downloads it and later responds to her great-grandpa, along with her comments or questions. Some of Harry's stories are true accounts from his own life and others are fiction.

• When young Elizabeth moved with her parents across the country, her Grandmother Karen was heartbroken and yet determined that she would continue to be an influence in Elizabeth's life. Every two weeks, she records a bedtime story on DVD and sends it to her granddaughter along with the book.

• "How much longer till we spend a week with Mamaw and Papaw?" eight-year-old Aaron asked. It was the highlight of his summer to spend a week on his grandparents' farm in Iowa, something he had been doing since he was five. It was the only time his grandparents saw him each year, and so Mamaw Pam would take pictures of their week together and put them on Facebook. After Aaron returned home he would be just a click away from reliving vacation memories.

Creative grandparents always find ways to stay in touch and express their love to grandchildren separated by the miles. This may involve buying stickers and sending them to a granddaughter who has a collection, or purchasing baseball cards or caps for another. Anything that says "We are thinking about you" strengthens the bond. As we mentioned before, it is wise to check with the parents to be sure the gift is appropriate and welcome.

One cardinal rule of effective grandparenting, whether from a distance or just across town, is to treat all grandchildren in an equitable manner. One child could be especially appealing to a grandparent. That's understandable. You may especially like the child's age, appearance, or behavior. However, it is crucial that you show love and attention as equally as you can. Even into adulthood, people never forget when grandparents obviously favored one child in a family over the others, and this can cause conflict among the siblings. Also, the favored one knows that something is out of kilter and does not appreciate the favoritism in the way the grandparents might imagine. If you are having difficulty understanding or appreciating the special qualities of each grandchild, we suggest that you read our book *The Five Love Languages of Children*.

What we have just said about favoritism applies to stepchildren as well. If you treat them as you do your own flesh and blood, you may be happily surprised to find that in time you feel close to them.

DIVORCE AND OTHER CHALLENGES
When Your Children Divorce

Divorce is one of the most crushing and destructive experiences an adult child can go through, and it does not disappear when one parent remarries. Divorce affects a child for life. Many children believe that they are responsible for their parents' divorce—if they had been better, their parents would have stayed together. Hurt, anger, and insecurity are the most common emotions felt by these children. In all their pain, grief, and disillusionment, they can find comfort in grandparents who are available with comforting arms.

But a word of caution: Grandparents often are experiencing their own pain, even grief, because of their children's divorce; and grandparents must learn to control their own emotions in order to help their grandchildren. When their world seems to be falling apart, these children reach for emotional support—that is, if the grandparents can retain a distance from the conflicts of the children's parents. In some cases, one set of grandparents is of no help to the children, because they are so heavily invested in blaming. At such a time, the young children should be the first consideration.

As grandparents, we need to recognize that we cannot solve the marital problems of our children, but we can love and care for our grandchildren. A listening ear, a caring hug, a prayer, and just being there all tell your grandchildren, "We care." Our grandchildren need to know that Grandma and Grandpa will be there for them, that we love them, and that we and our feelings won't change. They also need to know that their parents both still love them and always will. As grandparents, we are in the best position to bring this assurance to them.

In the midst of divorce, our grandchildren may bring questions to us. Answering these questions is usually difficult because we need to use caution. It is helpful to remember that most children don't want specific answers, but just want to express their feelings in a safe place. And yet, we can't ignore direct questions about the parents and the divorce. It is wisest to give the least possible amount of information. If they ask again, give just a tiny amount more. Also, there are some questions that only the parents should answer. The important role for grandparents is to be loving, caring, assuring, and giving of full attention.

While you may be concentrating on your grandchildren, you are clearly concerned for your son or daughter who is going through the divorce. You may be angry at what you consider to be their wrong behavior, or you may feel sympathetic because of "the way they have been treated." In most divorces, the blame is not all on one side. Both partners have likely failed in their efforts to understand and to give unconditional love to each other. Most misbehavior in marriage grows out of an empty love tank. Many spouses have never learned how to meet each other's need for love. When this goes unmet, we tend to be our worst selves.

While you cannot solve your children's problems or be a marriage counselor, you can recommend counseling and perhaps pay for it. You can make available some books that may help them put things back together. We recommend two books by Dr. Chapman that many couples have found helpful, *The Five Love Languages* and *Hope for the Separated: Wounded Marriages Can Be Healed.*

When Your Children Remarry

Many family circles are enlarging as young adults marry for the second time, and even for the third, bringing new children into grandparents' lives. With 80 percent of divorced people remarrying, many grandparents are finding that someone new is now helping to raise the grandchildren. As a grandparent, you have a concern for your grandchildren's well-being, yet at the same time must realize that your children have to be free to make their own decisions. Once your son or daughter has chosen to remarry, you need to accept that decision and seek to relate positively to the new spouse. If children from a former marriage are present, the new spouse has also become a new stepparent.

Even in the best of stepfamily situations, there is bound to be some tension, as the children are divided in their loyalties and are trying to adjust to new authority figures and siblings. Children may blame the new stepparent for all their problems, from the failure of the first marriage to the remarriage, and the confusion of moving. Also, children may blame their own parent for the breakup of their home, and also for marrying someone new. Grandparents can be points of stability and comfort when children are going through hard times.

Sometimes a grandparent receives signals that suggest the new stepparent is ignoring or mistreating a grandchild. The grandparent wants to intercede. If you should ever discover that the stepparent is behaving in an abusive way, you certainly have the right and responsibility to speak up on behalf of the children. But, how and to whom you speak is important. It is best if your adult child can take initiative to confront the abusing spouse about the issue. Your role may be to encourage and support your child. If your child is emotionally or mentally unable to do this, you may want to contact the national center for reporting physical abuse and ask for suggestions on what action you should take.

Being a step-grandparent is not easy, and yet as such, you are in a wonderful position to help the entire family. The more cordially you can relate to your adult child's new spouse, the better it will go with your new grandkids. If you can just be relaxed and patient, your relationship with your new step-grandchildren will probably develop naturally. It is rare that a grandparent does not eventually develop a loving bond with every grandchild, step or not. One thing you can do is to get acquainted with the other grandparents of the step-grandchildren. This will foster bonds for later cooperation and can also prevent problems.

With the tremendous increase in family disruption, grandparenting and step-grandparenting has become a vital area of helping and supporting your adult child. Many grandchildren are caught in a web of change, confusion, and bewilderment with little, if any, emotional guidance. Grandparents are often in the best situation to provide the emotional and even spiritual nurturance the children need.

When Grandparents Become Parents

Perhaps the most unusual situation grandparents may encounter is when they become parents again—rearing grandchildren on a temporary or permanent basis. This phenomenon is growing. A 2010 Pew survey found that 1 in 10 American children are now being raised by grandparents—or 2.9 million children. This represents a 30 percent increase since 1990. The rise directly parallels the Great Recession of 2007–2009 and mirrors a larger increase of multigenerational households. Thirty-four percent of grandparent caregivers are single.[3] In addition to economic factors, other causes include divorce, death of one or both parents, child abuse, physical addiction, and teenage pregnancy. Many grandparents are taking their children and grandchildren into their homes after a divorce, and others have the entire responsibility for raising one or more grand-children.

The number of those assuming complete care of their grandchildren has grown so fast that there are now several organizations and support groups to help them. One of these is Grandparents as Parents. According to its founder, Sylvie de Toledo, "Grandparents who find themselves taking the place of their adult children as parents are often bewildered and depressed by how their lives have changed."

There is no doubt that the grandparents' lives are radically changed. Their empty nest fills up, retirement dreams are postponed or forfeited, and their savings often dwindle. The emotional impact can also be severe, as grandparents feel trapped, powerless, frustrated, resentful, alienated, and guilty. The guilt can come from a sense that they failed in raising their own children and are now reaping the results in their grandchildren. All of this is happening at a time in their lives when they need order and stability. In some cases, the pressure can lead to depression that must be professionally treated.

If you are in this situation, you may find help through a support group in your community. Look on local government websites for "senior" resources, or check the AARP website (aarp.org), which has information on grandparents raising grandchildren. They may be able to assist you in locating a support group in your area and also answer questions about custody, health insurance, welfare benefits, and other issues that you face.

You should feel free to ask for the help that you need, not only from government agencies but also from your church and community groups. You may find people who would be glad to volunteer some time and support that will give you a needed lift. During your later years you can find strength to help you bring guidance and love to your grandchildren.

MEETING your own NEEDS

Someone has said that when children are little, they step all over your feet, and when they are older, they step all over your heart. The rigors of raising children can be extremely draining, physically, emotionally, and financially. By the time children reach young adulthood, many parents feel depleted. Parenting can be hazardous to your health.

"I thought that by this time we would be living on easy street, enjoying the fruit of our labors," one father said. "Instead, we have spent all of our retirement funds on lawyers, trying to keep our son out of jail. Now we've sold our house and moved to a smaller place, to reduce our monthly bills. If anything else happens, I don't know what we'll do. We're at the end of our rope."

Another couple has six grandchildren from two adopted daughters who have married men who don't like to work any more than is necessary to later draw unemployment checks. The husbands know how to work the system. The parents are caught in a hard place—they want to make sure their grandchildren are taken care of, but they don't think they should be supporting the young families.

When real emergencies or unavoidable problems assail their grown children, many parents feel bound to help. Sometimes the situation is not even due to ill-advised behavior; the child has an illness or disability. Whatever the problem or its cause, the long-term toll on parents can be major. Though the parents do care about the struggles of their children, they may have little strength, emotional energy, or money. Often the parents find their reserve tanks are empty.

CONSERVE YOUR RESOURCES

We parents, who naturally love our children, want to help. But how much can we do? How much should we do? Like the pink Energizer bunny who keeps going and going and going, we may keep giving and giving and giving. But unlike the rabbit, we may soon find our energy reserves drained. Wise parents recognize that physical, emotional, and financial resources always have limits.

The most common problem in parenting your adult child is overreacting to a crisis in the child's life. Parents may spend many resources trying to help the child through the crisis, only to find six months later that they are embroiled in yet another crisis. It is important that parents manage their physical and material resources prudently, so that they can be available to their children when there is real need.

Jill and Mark wish that someone had helped them understand this reality earlier in their relationship with their son, Brent. Unknown to them, he developed an alcohol addiction during his college years, but was able to finish his studies and earn a degree. When he entered the workforce, Brent was overwhelmed by the stresses of corporate life and sought relief in alcohol. He told himself and others, "I just need something to help me unwind at night." He wouldn't admit that he was an alcoholic.

In his first two years of work, Brent had three different jobs, always quitting just before he was about to be fired. Between jobs, his parents supported him by paying his rent and giving him a living allowance. Each time Brent would sober up long enough to find a new job, but within a year he was unemployed again.

When he quit his third job, his parents forced him into an expensive treatment center, for which they paid. Two weeks after he was released, he was drunk. This time his parents were so exasperated that they wrote him off, telling him that he was no longer welcome in their home until he got his life straightened out. The stress had been just too much for Jill and Mark. Both had medical problems and were emotionally depleted.

The story might have been different had they asked, as soon as they knew Brent had a problem, "What is the best way to help him?" This might have led them to admit their lack of knowledge about alcoholism and their need for outside help. Jill and Mark might have attended an Al-Anon meeting for family members of alcoholics, where they would have found good information and a supportive group. They would likely have made wiser decisions, conserved their financial resources until Brent was ready to benefit from a treatment program, and learned positive steps toward preserving their physical and emotional health.

Too many parents make the mistake of trying to deal with the crises of their adult children, without reaching out to others who have gone through similar experiences. When they do not seek available help, parents often lose themselves while trying to save their children. Many an older couple has ended up divorcing each other after having expended all their energies trying to help their adult children and failing to nurture their own relationship.

GIVE YOUR CHILD FREEDOM TO MATURE

Remember that your young adult child must live his own life, and that means solving his own problems. If you step in, you short-circuit the process of your child's emerging maturity. Your caring role is to give love, acceptance, encouragement, and guidance when requested. Many parents find this more difficult than stepping in to solve the problem.

As we have suggested in other chapters, it is crucial that you set boundaries for what is and is not acceptable behavior in the family setting. Once these boundaries are established, family members can hold one another accountable to staying within them. That often means allowing a child the freedom to take whatever course of action seems appropriate, even in a time of crisis. That there is an emergency does not negate the fact that the child is an adult.

Parents whose children are going through crises must maintain the balance between self-preservation and self-sacrifice. That, of course, can be a major challenge. On the one hand, we want to help them, for the noblest of all callings is the one to serve. And we can serve those we love—but always within limits. On the other hand, we must maintain our own health. Interestingly, Jesus of Nazareth, recognized by Christians and many non-Christians as the world's greatest example of a loving leader, once said He "did not come to be served, but to serve."[1] His life was characterized by self-sacrifice for the benefit of others. However, those who recorded His life indicated that at various times Jesus chose to withdraw from the crowds and retreat to a secluded spot for rest and prayer. Restoring His own physical and spiritual strength was important to Him; so it should be for us.

GUARD YOUR WELL-BEING

Your body requires proper maintenance. Without nutritious food, moderate exercise, and adequate sleep, your body can succumb to illness, disease, and possibly premature death. Do not allow your children's problems to keep you from the essentials for staying physically healthy.

The same is true of emotional health—you cannot ignore your own emotional needs and still expect to give continued help to your children over the long haul. For example, your own need for love requires that you spend time enriching your marriage and/or your relationship with family and friends. Your need for order or structure means that you will set boundaries both on yourself and your children. Your need for recreation and relaxation is fully as important as your desire to help your children.

One mother who realized this truth once told us: "I do water aerobics three times a week. If I didn't, I couldn't continue to help my son and his wife as they cope with the trauma of his cancer." Attending the symphony, doing physical exercise, mowing the grass, fishing, playing golf, and scores of other activities divert the mind, emotions, and body from otherwise overwhelming stresses.

Some parents feel guilty enjoying themselves when their children are in painful crises. However, becoming emotionally obsessed with the problems of adult children can bring one to a point of emotional exhaustion where they are no longer able to help at all. Therefore, regard your times of recreation as essential to your emotional health, as essential as food is to your physical health.

Also maintain your spiritual health. Your spiritual nature is often expressed in your desire for significance. Deep within all of us is a motivation to live in such a way as to make an impact on generations to come and to invest in things that count beyond the grave. Materialism is not an adequate base to satisfy these yearnings for ultimate significance. It is those yearnings for significance—inherently a spiritual quest—that motivates our noblest efforts at doing good in the world.

Most people know that the idea of significance is meaningless if there is not some ultimate authority that determines what is noble or ignoble, what is truly significant. For those in the Jewish and Christian traditions, the road to ultimate authority has led to the God of the Old and New Testaments, who from the dawn of man's creation has reached out to relate to His creatures. They believe that God revealed His moral law in the Bible. Those in the Christian tradition also believe God has sent as the Messiah Jesus Christ, who demonstrated what significant living is all about and how it may be obtained. In both traditions, Jews and Christians agree that taking time to establish and maintain our relationship with God is vital to maintaining spiritual health.

The authors believe that personal, regular times with God, through praying, reading Scripture, and meditating upon it, are exercises that feed the soul. This daily "quiet time" with God can become a healthy way of life, as important to our spiritual nature as food, exercise, and sleep are to the body.

For many who did not grow up in a religious tradition, a crisis in the life of one of their adult children or in their own lives often will awaken the reality of their need for spiritual help. For example, alcohol and drug addiction has led thousands of people to acknowledge two of the Twelve Steps of the Alcoholics Anonymous program: "Came to believe that a Power greater than ourselves could restore us to sanity. Made a decision to turn our will and our lives over to the care of God as we understood Him."[2] Such a discovery has been the beginning of a whole new dimension of life for these adults. They are not ashamed of the spiritual comfort they receive. Instead, they have acknowledged their need for God and found it a welcome first step in filling the spiritual void with which they have lived.

MEND YOUR RELATIONSHIPS

Year by year, we all face more stress. With our rapidly changing society, we need to learn to maintain ourselves better as we grow older. If we fail to give a high priority to our own well-being, we will have less energy and will feel more disillusioned. This leads to a loss of perspective about ourselves, our relationships, and life itself. Such loss of perspective can happen to any of us if we do not replenish ourselves physically, emotionally, and spiritually. Part of this self-nurture is to resolve issues that have the power to drag us down and plague us for years and even decades—issues that make us feel guilty, depressed, lonely, discouraged, or unworthy.

Those issues usually are related to the most basic elements of our lives and to the people who are or have been the closest to us. The issues often include the mistakes we have made in our own parenting. They can also include the mistakes our own parents made in their parenting of us—actions and attitudes that left us hurting with a pain that continues.

Most people have some mending to do on both sides, and we suggest that you look first to the hurts from the past. Many assume that those hurts will just evaporate, but that is not the case. The anger and hurt can stay with us at some level of consciousness until the day we die, unless we genuinely deal with the persons and actions that caused the pain. We will look at three ways to resolve the hurts of the past: (1) returning home, (2) writing letters, and (3) considering forgiveness.

1. Returning Home

James's father was an alcoholic who was emotionally severe with his children. He continually criticized them and was totally unloving. His mother was a passive woman who simply looked on as the father raged and ranted and put her down as well. James left home right after high school graduation, glad to be away from the two people he despised. After he served four years in the army, he got a scholarship and went to college and then on to graduate school, earning a PhD in psychology. During all these years, he went home only when necessity demanded it, such as the marriage of his sister.

While working on his graduate degree, James began to realize that for his own mental health he needed to mend his relationship with his parents. When he was thirty-five years old, he decided to return home by himself to visit and try to repair some of the brokenness. Driving to his hometown, he thought, *Perhaps I've been too harsh toward my parents. I wonder if my reactions had merely been those of an immature teenager. I wonder . . .*

The first evening James was home, things were going well. As the three of them watched television together, he was feeling comfortable and thinking what a good idea coming home had been. Mom, Dad, and James were seated watching an old sitcom when a woman on the show exclaimed, "This is my fifty-fifth birthday today!"

"What a coincidence," James's mother then said. "I'm fifty-five too." To which his father replied, "Yeah, but look at the difference."

Suddenly James felt the old nauseating feelings that he hoped he had left behind. He hated his dad's cruel gibe. He realized then that mending his relationship with his parents was not going to be that easy. He nearly gave up his plan, except that he had become a Christian since leaving home and had prayed often about his painful past. James decided to stay, and the next day he engaged his father in a conversation about his own childhood.

It was an eye-opener. As they talked, James discovered that his father had had a cruel mother who physically abused him and his two siblings.

He also learned that his father had been frequently ridiculed by his peers because of his exceptionally small stature. He began to realize what a difficult life his father had had. This gave him some understanding of his dad's poor self-esteem and his inability to show affection.

James did the same with his mother. In her case he was surprised by the underlying intelligence that she had kept hidden beneath her retiring personality. James had never been able to respect the way his mother would not exert herself against the bad treatment of her husband. As they talked at length, he discovered that she had years before taken the civil service examination and passed it with such high scores that she was given an excellent job with the Internal Revenue Service, and became one of the first six women IRS agents. Knowing that enabled him to respect her in a way he never had before.

That one trip, of course, did not in itself enable James to completely change his feelings and attitudes toward his parents, but it got things started. He kept in touch with them, and continued to consider what he had learned about them. He prayed about his relationship with his parents and talked to his wife and close friends about it. Gradually, James gained control of his anger and resentment and eventually came to a point that thinking of his parents did not bring feelings of hurt and bitterness. This took months and was not an easy time for James.

Finally he was able to forgive his parents for the pain that they had caused him and his siblings. This had a wonderful liberating effect for James. And, best of all, it gave him a new freedom in his own parenting, so that he is now able to be and do for his children what his own parents never gave to him and his siblings. And, when his parents died, he was profoundly thankful that he had dealt with those old issues while they were still alive.

James now watches some of his friends trying to cope with childhood issues and wishes they would take the same kind of reconciling measures that he did. Those unable to talk with their parents, to gain a better understanding of their lives, may be able to find an older relative or friend who can help.

You can return home again, and you can work toward knowing your own parents better. Deeper understanding and even reconciliation are possible. There are no guarantees, of course. But an open mind and a forgiving spirit can pave the way to objectively view your past—and your parents' past.

In James's case, a man who became a Christian was able to resolve painful issues with non-Christian parents. As counselors, we have met adults who suffered at the hands of Christian parents. We have known numerous people whose Christian parents have done many onerous acts in the name of God. This includes teaching their children, primarily by example, to scorn, blame, "fudge" (lie), despise, condemn, even abuse other family members. Some of these parents twist the Bible as they deal with their children, to place blame where none is due.

Can children in such relationships find healing? These are especially difficult relationships, but any effort is well worth it, for both parents and adult children. To carry a burden of anger, resentment, or bitterness is crushing and often debilitating. Finding pathways toward healing, peace, and forgiveness is a matter of grace, God's grace. It is important to God that we find that grace. Ask Him and He will help you.

2. Writing Letters

Another way to resolve deep hurts from the past is to write letters to your parents. The purpose of this is to get in touch with deep and possibly buried feelings. Putting those feelings on paper makes it much easier to see them accurately and then deal with them. First, you should release your negative feelings such as anger, hurt, and frustration. This may be difficult if you have suppressed them for a long time. You may be tempted to skip to positive feelings before releasing your negative ones, yet it is crucial that you be honest with yourself; everyone has some negative feelings toward their parents. Because the letter is not intended to be mailed, you can be fully honest with what you write. And, you can take all the time you need to process those feelings that you may have forgotten. If you find yourself crying and lamenting over what happened so many years ago, go ahead and release all of the hurt.

When you have spent adequate time dealing with the negative feelings, write another letter to each parent focusing on the positive. Again, don't be in a hurry.

You may decide that one of your letters would be appropriate to actually mail. Such correspondence can be an inexpensive way to communicate when distance, finances, and schedule make a return home impractical. You may find that letter writing is a good way to improve your relationship with your parents, and to keep communications positive.

Letter writing is rapidly becoming a lost art that needs to be revived, though email has encouraged more written correspondence. One caution in sending letters or email, however: Be careful not to send the correspondence until you are ready to do so; wait awhile and review for tone and word choice. Words could be easily misunderstood, yet written words are much easier to examine before transmission, and they're easier to talk about later.

3. Considering Forgiveness

When you think that you have exhausted the feelings regarding your parents, at least for the time being, it is time to consider forgiving them. Yes, *consider forgiveness*, because it must be done when you are ready. It is not simply saying that you have forgiven them; it requires letting go of the hurt. The act of forgiveness seldom takes place instantaneously.

Marsha had been sexually abused by her father. This had greatly affected her sexual relationship with her husband. At the urging of her husband, she went for counseling and soon gained insight into what had happened. Marsha knew she had to confront her father and deal with what had taken place so long ago.

One day they met; Marsha calls their dialogue "the most difficult conversation I have ever had." She told her father how the memories of those days brought her deep pain. How they had distorted her attitudes toward sex. How she had entered counseling to find help. How she was beginning to find healing. Then Marsha said that she wanted to offer him forgiveness if he wanted to be forgiven.

"That was the first time I ever saw my father cry," she said. "He told me that he had wanted to ask my forgiveness many times, but was too embarrassed to do so.

"I assured him that I did forgive him. I also told him that I was going to share this with Mom, because I had held a lot of resentment toward her through the years for letting this happen.

" 'I know this may cause some problems between the two of you,' I said, 'but you also need to deal with it. It has been hidden long enough. It may be painful, but I believe you will have a better relationship with Mom when the two of you work this out.' "

Marsha's conversation with her mother was equally difficult, but she knew it had to be done. She expressed her thoughts and feelings of resentment toward her mother. "I know that I should have shared this with you years ago," she said. "I'm sorry that I carried resentment around all these years." Marsha asked the questions she had wanted to ask for so long. She said the things she had always wanted to say.

Her mother responded first with shock, then anger toward her husband. Then she asked Marsha's forgiveness for the indirect role she played in not recognizing what was going on. Marsha embraced her mother for the first time in many years. And she forgave her mother.

The long road to recovery begins with confrontation and forgiveness. Once we have forgiven parents for past failures, we are free to begin to develop trust and restore friendships. Fortunately, Marsha's parents got the counseling they needed, and their marriage was renewed.

But what if parents, when confronted, deny that they did anything wrong? That often happens. Or what if parents are already deceased? In both cases the approach is the same: You release them to God who judges rightly, and you release to God (who knows and understands) your anger and bitterness.[3]

We cannot erase all the scars from past hurts, but we can experience freedom from the bondage of bitterness. The freedom comes by forgiving our parents. Forgiveness is the higher road; it opens the way to reconciliation and closeness, and it releases us from bitterness.

Such forgiveness is taught in the New Testament, which says a Christian can and should forgive because he has been forgiven. The Christian message is simple: A holy, righteous God wanted to find a way to maintain His commitment to justice yet forgive the human offender. His solution was to send Jesus, who lived a perfect life and yet paid the ultimate penalty for all sin—death. Therefore God can and does forgive all who will accept His forgiveness. Having experienced God's forgiveness, people are expected to forgive those who wrong them. The best-known prayer in the Bible includes the words: "Forgive us our debts, as we also have forgiven our debtors."[4] Forgiving our parents for past failures not only helps them, but it gives us a new freedom to face the future unfettered by the hurt, anger, and bitterness of the past.

Releasing our feelings and forgiving our parents gives us new insight into our own present relationship with an adult child. We have all heard the saying, "There is no such thing as a perfect child or a perfect parent." All parents have made mistakes, and all children have suffered in some way because of them. No one has come through childhood completely unscathed. It is impossible to live with another person without some conflict and misunderstanding, and that is not all bad. To lead a normal life in society, everyone must learn to express himself and make his feelings and wishes known, and learn to get along with others. Being able to accept differences is part of creating strong relationships.

The better we learn these lessons about conflict, the healthier, stronger, and more flexible we will be. Some people are easier to get along with than others. Unfortunately, we did not have a choice in our parents' personalities. Family life should be a time of learning to accept and respect differences, to live with varying perspectives. We can learn to tolerate those who irritate us, even cooperate with and negotiate with them. A favorite pearl of wisdom is this: "True intimacy comes from resolved conflict." This great truth is nowhere more applicable than in the parent-child relationship.

Most mistakes made by parents can be mended and forgiven. We have seen adult children accept their parents' apologies and genuinely forgive them for serious abuses. Of course, in doing so, the children were far more blessed than the parents. For the first time in their lives, the adult children were freed from the agony, pain, and distraction from which they suffered since childhood.

Of course, as parents, we must at times ask forgiveness of our children. It is better to do this before they reach adulthood. Think of the years of pain that could have been avoided if Marsha's father had taken the initiative to confess his wrong to her and ask forgiveness. His embarrassment would have been a small price to pay for the emotional healing, and his asking forgiveness could have alleviated years of estrangement. Not all of our failures are as detrimental as sexual abuse, but when we wrong our children, the results always are negative. Admitting our failures and asking our young adults to forgive us is the road to removing emotional barriers.

We suggest that such confessions always be made face-to-face if possible. If geographical distance is a problem, a letter is probably better than a phone call. The letter allows for reflection and time for a reasoned response.

If you have younger children who still live at home, admit your failures as soon as you become aware of them. Usually young children readily forgive parents who are honest enough to admit their failures. Such honest confession opens communication by making you approachable. It also sets an excellent example of humility and confession of mistakes. The child increases her respect for the parent and learns to forgive as well.

Some parents are not fully aware of the impact their mistakes had on their children. After they realize what they have done, and that all parents have made mistakes for which they need to confess to their children (and to God), they are then able to find relief from guilt and experience the peace they have longed for.[5]

RECONCILING WITH YOUR ADULT CHILD

You can make the necessary repairs in your relationships—not only with your parents, but also with your adult child. In most cases, your child will be out of the home. Therefore, the first step may be to write a letter in which you express how much you love and appreciate her. You can then explain some of your problems in being the parent you wish you could have been. You may also share the mistakes you know you have made. It is here that you can ask for her forgiveness and tell her of the love you will always feel toward her.

If your child accepts your letter, it is important that the two of you talk together about the past and mend your relationship in ways that will work for the future. Of course, if your child is still at home and you are aware of a fractured relationship you have caused, you can ask for forgiveness in person. But the need to then dialogue about the past still will be necessary, and the two of you also will need to work on ways to strengthen the relationship for the future.

RESPONSES BY YOUR ADULT CHILD AND YOU
What Your Child May Do

Regardless of the response you receive, you will know that you have done what a caring parent would do. This will ease your sorrow and guilt if your adult son or daughter rejects your heartfelt letter or personal confession and request for forgiveness. However, very few children will reject a letter of confession, remorse, and compassion. If there has been some overwhelming trauma between you and your child, it may be best to seek help from someone who is qualified to help you. You could seek professional counseling first for yourself, and later, if appropriate, for other family members. For a broader scope of this subject, we recommend Shauna Smith's excellent book, *Making Peace with Your Adult Children*.

In this process, your child may voice complaints about the past that seem confrontational. He may be angry or defensive. He may actually believe you are not deserving of forgiveness. How should you respond to this confrontational tone?

What You Should Do

Our caution is, do not fall into the trap or employ any of the negative strategies shown below. Instead, handle the grievances in a mature and positive way. This also means that you will not become defensive. In her book, Smith has included scenarios illustrating twenty common responses of parents to confrontations by their adult children.

COMMON RESPONSES TO CONFRONTATIONS BY ADULT CHILDREN

Counterattack	Self-Defense
Call to Higher Authority	Implication That the Child Is Crazy
Avoidance of the Subject	Cliché-Quoting
Philosophical Statements	Minimizing the Child's Experience
"Ungrateful Child"	Denial of the Truth
Pain Comparison	Sarcastic Response
Shifting of Blame	Giving Unsolicited Advice
Defense of Someone Else	Righteous Pose
Walking Away	Humiliation or Abasement of Self
"You're Saying That to Hurt Me"	"It Was Good Enough for Me"[6]

Have a Healthy, Positive Outlook

As you seek to increasingly relate to your child in healthy adult ways, think of the ways you relate to persons you respect and admire. You ask their opinions and discuss mutual interests with them. You invite them to activities that are important to you and to your associates. You want to move toward a healthier perspective toward life—a perspective that gives a positive mental outlook and emotional reaction to life, and especially to the future.

The way you regard the future is either more optimistic or pessimistic. You probably aren't fully in either camp, but tend in one direction or the other. An optimist is more likely to ignore facts that are negative, and has an overly favorable view of life. A pessimist first sees factors that are primarily negative and has an overly unfavorable view of life. It is generally easier for an optimist to have a balanced perspective on life. We recommend that perspective. It will aid you in dealing with the tensions in your relationships with family and coworkers. Pessimists are more prone to depression, and that can aggravate the pessimism even more.

However, there is hope for us all. One study conducted at Ohio State University found that those of us who are more inclined to pessimism—or "realism"—don't have to completely change our personalities. All we have to do is avoid pessimism. Says psychologist Susan Robinson-Whelen, senior author of the OSU study: "Just because people don't always see the bright side of everything doesn't mean they expect bad things to happen to them."[7] That is encouraging. And research at Case Western University found that only 2 percent of people were true optimists. "Bottom line: you don't have to live sunny-side up all the time," observes writer Barbara Smalley, "but you *do* have to banish pessimism from your life. And that's easier than you think."[8]

When tempted to be pessimistic, we parents should do the following: (1) consider the objective evidence rather than just our feelings; (2) not blame ourselves when things go wrong; (3) make a list of our accomplishments and review it; (4) take care of ourselves; and (5) "fake it till we make it."[9]

We have more control over our lives than we often think. We can make choices that impact us and those around us in very positive ways. We don't have to just wait and see what turns up. We don't have to feel victimized by life, even by those curveballs our children at times throw our way.

We need to be at our best for the task and privilege of parenting, at any age. Parenting adult children is just as important as parenting the little ones, but it is different and we are learning as we go. If we want to do our best, we have to be our best.

BUILDING a
confident, growing
RELATIONSHIP

We asked several parents, "How would you describe your present relationship with your young adult child?" Their answers varied.

• Gail, mother of a seventeen-year-old son: "Things have been better. Three nights this week, he has been out past his curfew. Right now there is a lot of tension between us."

• Bob, father of a twenty-three-year-old son: "I'd say our relationship is good. He has his own apartment now, so I don't see him every day, but we talk at least once a week. I think we are doing well."

• Tim, father of a nineteen-year-old son: "Not very good. Our son has lots of problems. He doesn't want to go to college and he hasn't been able to keep a job. I don't like the people he hangs out with—I think they are a bad influence on him. Our relationship is very strained right now."

• Liz, mother of a twenty-five-year-old married daughter: "We have a wonderful friendship. She is happily married and expecting her first child. We have fun shopping together for baby things. I am so happy for her and excited about becoming a grandmother."

How would you describe your relationship with your child? Your answer to this question will reveal where you need to start if you desire a growing relationship. Understanding where you are will give you some clues as to where you need to go.

Human relationships are dynamic and always changing. Your relationship with your adult child is growing closer or more distant; becoming more satisfying or more troublesome; getting better or worse. This means that you need to constantly work at the relationship to maintain it or change it.

Many parents fail to let the relationship mature as their children become adults, but continue to treat the young people as if they were children. This can lead to serious conflicts and can actually promote immature behavior, even though this is the last thing the parents intend.

In this chapter, let's consider how we can have positive, growing relationships with our children—even a friendship. We must qualify this goal, however: Parents can't create a good relationship with a child, but they can help create a climate in which the relationship can develop.

OUR POWER TO INFLUENCE

Too many parents minimize their own power to create that positive climate; they blame all the difficulties on the child's behavior. "If Bridget would only stop dating that miserable creature, we could get along well again," one father said. Such a statement assumes that the parent is powerless until the child makes a change. This attitude of blame has led many parents to believe the myth "There's nothing else I can do." Once they believe this myth, a fractured relationship may continue indefinitely.

Far more productive is this parental attitude: "I do not like the present behavior of my adult child. I know that I can't change that behavior, but I can and will seek to have a positive influence on him."

Your attitude, words, and behavior do influence your child every time you are together. When your child walks into the room and you drop your newspaper, look him in the eye and say excitedly, "Hi, Jeff. You're looking mighty healthy today. What's going on?" You have created a climate that promotes communication. But, if you merely toss a quick glance in his direction and say, "You need a haircut, boy," you have erected a major roadblock. He may walk out of the room mumbling, "Excuse me. I'm sorry I showed up."

As parents, we must take responsibility for our own power of influence and stop blaming our children for the bad relationship. We are older and should be more mature. Our children are on the front end of life, still trying to learn. We can go a long way in creating a good climate in which that learning can take place.

WHAT CONFIDENT PARENTS DO

We all long to be confident parents. Although we will never completely reach the goal, the closer we come to it, the better our children will develop. We need to continue to grow in our parenting as our children become adults. Unfortunately, many parents do not make appropriate changes so that they can reach a truly rewarding adult-to-adult relationship with their children. But when parents and adult children behave in a mature manner, all of them can experience a new meaning and joy in life.

Confident parents do all in their power to help their children mature. They place genuine importance on their children's feelings and thoughts, and let them know that those opinions and feelings are deeply important. They want to come to really understand their children. They want to know how much guidance and freedom their children need. Parents who are sensitive to their children in these ways often come to the wonderful realization of how deeply they respect and value their adult children as friends.

"Mom is one of my best friends," says twenty-seven-year-old Andrea. She enjoys spending time visiting her mom, Cheryl. "We talk openly and we do lots of things together." Cheryl described some of the things the two do together: "Oh, we go shopping. . . . We enjoy going to a movie and discussing it afterwards. Last month we attended a conference on 'women's issues.' We had a great time together. I enjoy getting her ideas on things. She is my link to understanding the younger generation."

Asked about her closeness to her mom, Andrea said after thinking a moment, "I think it's because Mom has allowed me to grow up. She doesn't treat me like a child. She does not try to tell me what to do. Because of that, I respect her ideas. In fact, I often ask her advice. I don't think I would do that if she tried to control me."

Cheryl is experiencing a parental joy some mothers never know. Confident parents *can* eventually have a friendship with their adult children. Confident parents can also set a goal that their children will become independent in the late teen years. To reach that goal, they give the children choices whenever possible, guiding them in making the best ones, so that their children will learn to take responsibility for their own behavior. This often means that they have let their children when younger take small risks, follow their own desires when these are within reason, and not be smothered by overprotection. When parents build up the possible dangers involved in small risks, they create fear and resentment in their children.

Confident parents are loving and supportive in letting their children take steps toward maturity. The goal, of course, is that these children will become self-assured, independent, and right-thinking adults.

It is common to view good parenting as a balance between love and discipline, but confident parenting is far more than that. Have you noticed the increasing numbers of problems with children who come from good homes? These parents have given much love and their discipline is handled adequately. But there is a problem—the way family members handle anger. Mishandling anger in the home results in two things: the children not knowing how to manage their own anger and their having attitudes against authority. Thus, confident parents rightly manage their anger, and they discipline out of love—and never while they are angry, when they may do or say things out of control.

THE JOURNEY TOWARD MATURITY

Confident parents let their adolescent and young adult children take risks and move toward maturity. They also understand that their children will pass through several stages on their way to maturity. Researcher

Michael Bloom has found five stages in the growth process to adulthood.[1] My own observations during more than thirty-five years of counseling parents and adolescents agree with his conclusions. The five stages on the road to maturity are:

1. Children begin to rebel against parental authority. In early adolescence, at about age twelve, children vacillate between needing restraint and freedom. This stage ends when the parents appropriately adjust their ways of handling the children, to accommodate this normal phase.

2. Children enter normal adolescent rebellion. They challenge house rules, place high interest on peer relationships, and begin to question their parents' values.

3. Children move on, to college, the military, or a job. Often this means they begin to live away from their parents. This is a time of separation with some sadness and grief.

4. Family members redefine themselves and their roles during this phase, as they see much less of each other. The parents find different outlets for their energies and the children discover their own values.

5. Adult-to-adult relationships develop, in which each person is seen as a separate and valued individual.

Most children progress fairly well until they reach stage two or three. When adolescence hits their homes, many parents make few adjustments in their way of interacting, and continue with the same parent–young child relationship. The parents often are unaware of what they are doing, but because the child hasn't gotten into any particular difficulties before adolescence, the parents have "gotten away" with their mistakes.

However, the parents are falling into traps or unfortunate styles of parenting (see below). Then, when they later see their mistakes, they feel guilty and often believe themselves to be failures. When their children are grown, many of these parents believe that there is no hope of making corrections or being reconciled with their children. Yet, in most situations, when parents realize their mistakes, there is time and opportunity to make corrections. They can get their adult children's development back on track.

Now that you have this new knowledge and awareness of the good and the bad, the positive and the negative, regarding your past relationship with your child, you have the opportunity to make things better. This is the time to get things straightened out, but this does not mean "fixing your adult child." Getting things straightened out means "fixing your *relationship* with your adult child." To do this, you need to look at your parenting style. We do not wish to be negative, but we need to point out these unhealthy styles of parenting. Ask yourself, "Have I practiced any of these styles?" We call these three styles *"parent traps."*

THREE PARENT TRAPS

Parent Trap 1: Overprotection

Parents who insist, "Let me do it for you," fall into parent trap number one. They want to do for their children what, perhaps, was not done for them. However, they do so much that their children never learn to do for themselves. Their "kindness" fosters a dependency that appears in several areas of life, the most obvious of which is financial. The young people grow up knowing little about the value of money and feeling low motivation to work. These are the "helicopter parents" we are hearing about in the media.

This dependency may also affect school performance, especially when a parent has been overly involved in homework assignments and term papers. The child is learning less and expecting someone else—a father or mother—to help. Such parents would have done better to say, "Let me show you how," and then to turn the task of doing over to the child. The child can also become dependent on others for skills needed for daily living. Some young people go off to college totally unable to care for themselves. If they then marry similarly handicapped persons, they will have major conflict in marriage, as they each expect the other to be responsible.

Overprotection is a stifling way to raise a child. Of course, we parents must be protective of our children, especially when they are young, but we also need to remember that we cannot always be there for them. We want to prepare them for a day when full independence comes, and that means working toward that goal. One secret is to let your children know that you are working together toward their independence. You want them to know that you intend for them to be ready. Such openness makes it more likely that adolescent children will be more cooperative with necessary restrictions.

Why do some fall into this parent trap? Overprotective parents usually accept one or two false beliefs. The first is that a child cannot make it without the parent's constant involvement. The second is that the parent cannot bear the thought of a child—even an adult child—having any pain or problems out in the real world. Ironically, this is most prevalent in parents who have had to survive great hardships and have emerged as competent people. Instead of realizing that their hardships are what made them strong and competent, they desire that their children have problem-free lives with no character-building trials. They forget that it takes preparation and training to be able to function and prosper in a world that is far from being user-friendly. Part of this training is to experience difficulty. There is no other way for children to learn to deal with the normal stresses of life.

This parenting style is very difficult to change, but the parent who recognizes the pattern needs to take responsibility for changing it, or their adult child will be dependent for a lifetime. The older the child, the more difficult to break the pattern. But failure to break the pattern will eventually result in greater pain for both.

Still, the pattern can be broken later, as the Garners would tell you. Steve and Lynda realized their dependency patterns with Monica only when their daughter had graduated from college. Prior to that, the Garners had paid all of Monica's college living expenses, including giving her a credit card and paying her bills. Every two or three weeks, she would come home from school for the weekend, bringing all of her dirty clothes for her mother to wash. Also, Lynda fixed her favorite meals when she was home.

The way Steve and Lynda saw it, they were just glad that Monica came home often; they felt thankful that they could take care of her expenses. They thought Monica respected them and felt as close to them as they did to her.

These feelings began to change, however, when Monica moved in with a friend after graduation. Her parents thought she was on her way to establishing her own lifestyle, but wondered why she continued to bring home her laundry. Several weeks later they got a call from Monica's roommate saying that Monica had not paid her part of the rent for the past two months, and had also borrowed money that she hadn't repaid. "I know you two are close to Monica," she said, "and I just thought that before this gets out of hand perhaps you could talk to her about it."

Steve and Lynda were shocked, and that night they had a long talk. They soon realized that their parenting style had not taught Monica to manage money or take responsibility. They knew that if they did not do something quickly, their daughter could be in serious trouble.

Meanwhile, Monica was struggling with the pressures of her new job. She knew that she was not doing well in handling her money, and she didn't respond well when her parents confronted her with what they had learned. Through her tears she said, "I feel like you're disappointed with me and don't trust me with money. I thought you wanted to do my laundry and to have me come for meals."

"We do want you to come over for meals, sweetheart," her father said. "We enjoy being with you, but we also want you to learn how to cook and do your own laundry. We realize that we have failed to teach you both of these things. About the money, it's not that we don't trust you but that we know now that we haven't given you any help in understanding how to manage money. We feel that this is an area of parenting where we have failed you."

After a few more rounds of words and tears trying to understand each other, they all agreed that some changes would be in order, for Monica's own good. However, she had been dependent on her parents for so long that her behavior patterns were not going to change quickly. In the early stages of their plan, Steve and Lynda rescued her a few times from financial situations, until they realized that this was not helping her. They had to allow her car to be repossessed if she failed to meet the monthly payments. This was very difficult for them, but they knew they could not rescue her again. In the beginning, Monica accused them of abandoning her.

Over the next months, Monica did learn how to handle her money, how to do her laundry, fix meals, and numerous other tasks that her parents had done for her. Eventually, she got another car, and even learned how to have routine maintenance done on it.

When she was twenty-six, Monica married a young man she met at work. He told Steve and Lynda how fortunate he was to be marrying a woman who knew where to go to get the oil changed, and he congratulated them on the wonderful job they had done in raising Monica. They smiled at each other and told their new son-in-law thank you. That night at home, they congratulated each other on the hard work they had done over the last three years in helping Monica become independent.

Parent Trap 2: Undermanagement

Parents who do not give enough management to their children's lives can be of various types. Some may seem distant and unapproachable, and not know how to care for their child's emotional needs. Many undermanage because they fear displeasing their children, even losing their love; some give little input because they dislike conflict. Others may be overly permissive; still others devote little time to their children's lives because of busy or long work schedules (which often leave them tired when they arrive home).

Those parents who seem distant usually grew up in homes where their own parents provided for physical needs but failed to relate to them on an emotional level. Consequently, they have little idea of how to develop such a relationship with their own children. These parents need to work toward understanding the value of emotional closeness with their children. Ideally, this would be done when the children are young, but it is never too late to learn.

For parents who realize that they have a distant relationship with their adult children, a change in lifestyle is called for. You can no longer do what you have always done if you want to minimize the weakness of this parenting style. If your problem is that you are too busy working or helping others, you need to slow down and begin connecting with your children.

Mark was one such parent. When he began to understand what he had done, he enrolled in a class on parenting teenagers so that he could connect better to his boys, ages thirteen and eighteen. Mark had been busy climbing the corporate ladder and had not been around for many of the boys' activities. When he started to notice that they did not come to him with their questions, but to their mother, it dawned on him that he had done little to develop a relationship with the boys.

Mark first talked with his wife about this and then with his sons, sharing with them his sense of having let them down. He told them: "To the best of my ability, I want to change this in the future. I love you very much and want the best for you. All the work I've done has been with you in mind, but that's no excuse for not spending more time with you."

The younger son, Josh, appreciated Mark's confession and said he wanted to spend more time with him. But Brad, a college freshman, was more tentative.

"Dad, I hear what you're saying, but as you know, I won't be here much longer," Brad said. "I would love to spend time with you, but I don't know when that will be possible."

Mark felt hurt, but he understood Brad's reaction and determined to spend more time with him. He attended all his soccer games at the university, and when Brad was home on weekends, he made sure that they spent time together. In the few years since Mark confessed to his sons that he had been uninvolved, both sons have developed a much closer relationship with their dad. Mark just wishes that his eyes had been opened earlier to the value of giving more time and attention to his children.

Those parents who are very permissive choose to be uninvolved, thinking that their children can do as they please—even in situations where direction, protection, or control is needed. These parents need to be more aware of what is appropriate freedom or responsibility for various age levels. Also, they need to be more cautious in a dangerous world.

Some types of undermanagement are not so obvious, especially in our increasingly competitive world. Today's young people require more guidance than young people of the past. As it becomes more difficult to find rewarding employment and to raise families in our technological world, older children need guidance in areas such as academic course selection, college preparation, career choices, and appropriate and healthy recreation.

Most parents who undermanage their children do so because they are confused about parenting and are afraid of displeasing their children, even losing their love. They either struggle with their own self-esteem or they misunderstand the true meaning of discipline. If you are having problems in either area, we recommend you read Ross's books *How to Really Love Your Child* and *How to Really Love Your Teenager*, especially the chapters on discipline. Discipline is actually an important way to demonstrate you love your children; such discipline, however, must be done with love and respect. In many situations requiring discipline you may feel confused and exasperated. Please remember, if you remain pleasant but firm, you will do well.

Some parents who undermanage their children simply hate conflict. When the children realize this, they are eager to take advantage of it. Remember, our children—and especially our adult children—know us better emotionally than we know ourselves. Even if we have an aversion to conflict, we must remind ourselves that our children need to learn good values and skills, many of which they may not encounter unless we provide the kind of direction we should.

Parent Trap 3: Overmanagement

With this parenting style, the parents are deeply involved with their children, devoting much energy to help their offspring learn and grow. Since the children's earliest years, the parents sought to give their children auditory and visual stimuli to develop their intellectual capacities. They gave lots of hugs and kisses and affirming words to meet the children's emotional needs. They attended all the ball games, piano recitals, and dance performances.

The description sounds very positive, doesn't it? Now, as their children move into adulthood, they intend to continue being good parents. The problem is that they fail to shift gears, and the young adults who are seeking independence feel dominated. Thus, they draw away from their parents, spending less time with them and asking less and less advice. This hurts the parents, who feel that their children are abandoning them.

The solution? Parents whose style is intense, hands-on management need to draw back, pray more and probe less, and give their children the freedom to make decisions on their own. The perimeters of freedom must be extended in sequential steps from little to much, as the children move from adolescence to adulthood.

Overmanaging a child can also mean handling the child with an authoritarian attitude, being a boss to the child; in a sense, playing God. It can mean giving orders as though the child were a Marine recruit. This is fine in the military, but no way to "train a child in the way he should go."[2] This approach may seem to work when the child is small, but it is really counterproductive. It does not teach a child to interact with you or others in healthy and meaningful ways. Therefore, you are depriving your child of the privilege of learning the skills of social interaction. She cannot learn to carry on pleasant small talk, an increasingly critical skill in today's world. She will be hampered in learning to make decisions and to think for herself. A child who is continually told what to do and how to think will struggle with learning how to manage life.

Overmanagement leaves the child no other emotional recourse than to become angry. Since there is little room for discussion or the teaching of verbal skills to handle the anger, the child's anger will emerge as antiauthority attitudes. The child probably will display antiauthority behavior toward parents, teachers, employers, and local authorities. Many Christian parents use the overmanagement approach to parenting, partly because they have been taught that this is what God desires. However, such an approach will backfire on them when the children reach adulthood.

Besides developing anger, the child reared by the overmanaging parental style will likely fail to learn to accept responsibility for his own behavior. We need to remember the old axiom "Two people cannot take responsibility for the same thing at the same time." The child must be given the opportunity to take responsibility for some of his behavior, even at an early age. And the amount needs to increase appropriately, or he will never learn how. All around us we see people who have never learned. They are perpetual victims. Everything is someone else's fault. A number of years ago a woman spilled a cup of McDonald's coffee on herself, scalding her legs. She showed questionable judgment by placing the hot cup of coffee on her lap as she drove away from the food-pickup window. It spilled. She sued the fast-food chain; she blamed McDonald's for serving the coffee too hot. Interestingly, the court agreed, ruling that she was the victim and awarding a king's judgment against McDonald's.

The negatives of this parent trap need not continue. Joe and Teresa had both had meddlesome parents who clearly overmanaged. When the couple married, they struggled to free themselves from the interference. When their own children reached adolescence, they began training them for independence, giving input but letting them wrestle with decisions. Throughout high school, they let their children make more and more of their own decisions. The week before sixteen-year-old Vincent got his driver's license, they sat down with him and let him help them decide the consequences if he were caught speeding or breaking other traffic laws. They were surprised at how mature his ideas were. Letting Vincent be a major player in deciding the consequences was teaching him how to make decisions.

When his first traffic offense happened six weeks later, Joe and Teresa did not overreact. They all knew what the consequences would be. Letting children make decisions and suffer the consequences or reap the benefits is a good way to teach them how to make wise decisions.

Parents who seek to teach their children to make decisions by allowing them the freedom to do so will likely minimize the tendency to meddle in the lives of young adults. They will "be there" for their children, but they will not dominate. One wise boundary many parents have set for themselves is not to give their married children advice unless requested. Sharing this self-imposed boundary with children before they marry is a good way to let them hold you accountable for staying within your boundary.

YOU CAN DO IT

It is crucial to understand that no one has done a perfect job with their children. Parenting is about the most difficult job in the world, and few of us have had any training in it. Yet, even if you had the best training in the world, there are still situations that no one can foresee, and some that almost no one can cope with well. Every family is different and every child unique. When we admit that we have made mistakes, and when we understand just how and when we misjudged, we can begin to do something about it.

Most parents have done something right. It is helpful to make a list of all the ways you have been a good parent. You should enumerate them, from the small acts to the most sacrificial, to help you see the whole picture. You want to focus on the complete relationship with your child, not only on what has gone wrong. Emphasize the positive aspects of your bond with your child and what you have done right.

A PARENT'S POSITIVE LOVE

We have emphasized that "confident parents are loving and supportive." Adult children are most open to the influence of those who love them. This is often why they are so receptive to the influence of peers and closed to their parents. Their friends give them acceptance and affirmation, and their parents may give them condemnation. Parents who wish to be a positive influence must focus on meeting their children's need for emotional love. But how can we parents make our children feel they are loved?

We do this by assuring our children in many ways "I love you, no matter what." At times, we may not like their behavior, but that doesn't mean we withhold our love. To do so is to love them "only if . . ." which is not true love. It is okay to tell your child, "I may not like what you are doing, but it will not keep me from loving you." This is true unconditional parental love.

Speak Your Child's Love Language

As you seek to meet your adult child's need for emotional love, it is important to realize that not everyone understands the same love language. What makes one person feel loved will not necessarily make another feel that way. Thus your child may not sense your love if you are speaking or expressing your love in a way (language) she doesn't understand. We believe that there are five basic languages of love and that each person will understand one of them more deeply than the other four. It is the parents' job to know the primary love language of their adult child and to give heavy doses of love in this language.

Here is a brief description of the five languages. (This is a summary of chapters 2–6 of our book *The Five Love Languages of Children.*) Each of these languages represents a different way you can express love. Again, your adult child will most sense your love when you speak her language (although our children need to receive expression of love in all five languages).

1. Words of Affirmation. You use words to build up or affirm the person. "You look nice today. . . . Thanks for feeding the dog. . . . I appreciate your bringing in the mail while I was gone. . . . Your car looks great. . . . I like your apartment." To the child whose love language is *words of affirmation,* all these statements express love. "Your boss must have really been impressed. This report looks super. . . . I'm proud that you are my son/daughter. . . . You are a wonderful parent to your babies." Such statements are appropriate words of affirmation for young adults.

2. Gifts. The bestowing of gifts is a universal language of love. A gift says, "He was thinking of me. Look at what he brought me." Phil remembered that his twenty-one-year-old son Darian collected Coke bottles when he was in junior high and still had the bottles stored in his apartment. During a business trip to Egypt, Phil bought Darian a Coke bottle. When he gave it to him on his return, Phil saw the biggest smile he had seen in years. The reason: To Darian, that gift said to him: "Dad remembered. He cares." Gifts need not be expensive; they may be as simple as a stone picked up on a hiking trail—or a fifty-cent Coke bottle. They are visual symbols that someone cares.

3. Acts of Service. This involves doing things that you know your child will appreciate. Cooking a favorite meal or dessert, repairing a mechanical device, keeping your son's dog or children while your daughter-in-law and he are on vacation, mowing their grass when he isn't feeling well, helping him fill out their income tax return—all of these are more than acts of kindness. They are speaking love on an emotional level, for they demonstrate that you care. And if this is your adult child's primary love language, such acts make your son feel really loved.

4. Quality Time. In spending quality time with your child, you are giving her your undivided attention, really giving a part of your life, so that she has all of you at that moment. Quality time may include taking a walk together or shopping or going to a movie together. The important thing is not the activity but being together. Conversations are part of most expressions of quality time. Conversations are enhanced by eye contact. Wise parents put down their book or newspaper or turn off the TV when their young adult starts talking. Such focused attention speaks volumes of love to the child.

5. Physical Touch. The language of physical touch may include a hug when the child comes for a visit, a pat on the back as he enters the room, sitting close enough to touch shoulders as you watch TV or a movie together, an arm on the shoulder as you serve him a soda. All of these express love through touch.

To learn ways to recognize your child's primary love language, see chapter 7 of *The Five Love Languages of Children.*

Requests and Suggestions

If you are expressing love to your child and keeping your child's love tank full, you probably know that *requests are more productive than demands.* No one likes to be controlled, and demands are efforts at controlling. Demands may get results, but they are almost always accompanied by resentment. "Brad, would you turn the TV down while I'm on the phone for the next several minutes, please?" is a request. "Brad, turn that television down while I'm on the phone" is a demand. Both may get results, or neither may; but the request tends to keep the relationship positive while the demand drives a wedge of resentment.

Therefore, demands should be reserved as a last-ditch effort to get the behavior we desire. We aren't suggesting that you should never demand anything of your young adult children, especially those who still live in your home. Just keep them as a last effort, not the first.

Requests should always be as specific as possible, since general requests are ambiguous and seldom get the desired results. "Would you help me clean the house?" is too general to be meaningful to a nineteen-year-old. Far better to request, "Would you please vacuum the carpet downstairs before you leave this morning?" This is clear, doable, and includes your desired time framework.

We would also recommend that you *give suggestions rather than proclamations.* "You need to get this application in today or you are not going to get the job" is a proclamation. It assumes that you know everything. "You know what I would suggest? That you try to get the application in today. I think that the earlier you get it in, the more likely you are to get an interview and perhaps the job" is a suggestion. Young adults tend to respond much more positively to suggestions than they do proclamations.

When we make God-like proclamations, our children are likely to dismiss them as, "The wind is blowing again," and not give serious thought to our proclamations. However, when we offer suggestions, we are acknowledging our humanity and limited experience. We are simply sharing our best thoughts, which they are more likely to receive as such, and give them due consideration.

HOPE FROM THE BIBLE

Some of us have forgotten how to be confident in a fallen world. Parenting has changed just as our world has changed. Our children have grown and we keep having to learn the next lessons.

By this time, we are well aware of the mistakes we have made and that we are far from perfect parents. And yet, we can go on to greater maturity and be ready to make the necessary changes for the future. And we can help our children move to maturity as well.

You can find inspiration, comfort, and confidence in parenting in the Bible. We encourage you to read the many promises it gives concerning our children. Two that come to our mind are "Children are a gift of the Lord, the fruit of the womb is a reward" and "The lovingkindness of the Lord is from everlasting to everlasting on those who fear [respect] Him, and His righteousness to children's children."[3]

Other verses of hope include Psalm 112:2; 138:8; Isaiah 44:3–5; 54:13; and Jeremiah 31:17. Such verses can sustain parents who are concerned and prayerful about their children.

leaving your CHILD
a positive LEGACY

Upon their deaths, most parents leave some material legacy to their children, whether money, clothes, furniture, or cars. Sometimes the legacy can be a small but meaningful gift. John, a fifty-four-year-old bricklayer, buried his seventy-eight-year-old father a year after his mother passed away. His father had lived in a nursing home for several years; his money had run out and he was on Medicaid for most of that time.

"Before he died," John recalled, "he told me he wanted me to have his wedding band. After his death, when I went to the nursing home, they gave me a bag with Dad's clothes. At the bottom was a small plastic bag containing his wedding band. Now that ring is on my dresser and I look at it every day and remind myself of Dad's faithful marriage to Mom for over fifty years. I think about all he did for me when I was young and I pray that I will be the kind of husband and father he was." John's words tell of a legacy far more valuable than material property, of which the ring was a symbol.

Matt's story is very different. The only child of his widowed father, Matt received everything his father had accumulated—over a million dollars in cash and stocks; two houses filled with valuable furnishings; cars, boats, and several rental properties. Matt's response? "I never really knew my father and have no idea what to do with all his stuff. He left my mother when I was thirteen and I didn't see him for five years. When I was ready for college, he agreed to pay for my expenses. From that point, we saw each other periodically over the next forty years, but we never had a close relationship. He was involved with one woman after another and I always felt that he didn't have time for me. My children knew him only as the grandfather who gave expensive Christmas gifts.

"If I had known him, I might appreciate all the stuff he left me. Of course, I can use the money, but the inheritance doesn't have any personal meaning for me."

MORE THAN MONEY

A legacy is an inheritance handed down from one generation to the next, something by which our descendants remember us. In a legal sense, a legacy is a deposition of personal property that is made by terms of a will, "something transmitted by or received from an ancestor or predecessor," according to *Merriam Webster's Collegiate Dictionary* (tenth edition). But its impact is usually deeper than material—our legacy will have a powerful influence on the lives of those who follow us. As we saw in the stories of John and Matt, the most important legacies are not monetary, but emotional, spiritual, and moral, and they center around the character of the person leaving them.

Legacies from the past affect a family's future. We all know families with longstanding reputations of good character—kindness, honesty, decency, upstanding behavior, and more. We all know fortunate people who inherited such a positive legacy from their parents and grandparents, and we can see the great advantages to them in terms of self-esteem and emotional well-being. On the other hand, we are aware of the handicaps borne by those who are plagued by a parent's negative legacy of character and behavior. While we like to believe that an individual can overcome any disadvantage, we all know that what has happened in our families can seem either a blessing or a curse on our lives.

A *Legacy in Personal Lives*

John and Nancy have been married thirty-five years. They have four children and three grandchildren. John came from a family with a poor legacy. His grandfather and father were alcoholics, and his father displayed no affection for his wife and children. John suffered in this household and decided to join the army immediately after high school.

His military experience was valuable, giving him the confidence he so lacked because of contact with his father. He now learned that he was competent and bright. After his tour ended, he entered college and did quite well. There he met Nancy, "the most beautiful woman I had ever seen," he recalls with delight. She was an exceptionally fine person, who was reared in a good family. The couple dated and soon married, and from her experiences of growing up in a healthy household, Nancy became a loving and supportive spouse. John loved her deeply and was profoundly appreciative of the sound parenting she had received. Nancy's mother and father had demonstrated to her what a family could and should be.

In Nancy's parents John found the family he had never had. Nancy's father took him golfing; her mother cooked John's favorite foods. The couple gave him the love and understanding he craved.

"When her father first gave me a hug," John remembers, "I didn't know how to respond. I had never been hugged by a man before. When her mother said 'I love you,' I went home and cried. That was the first time anyone had ever said those words to me."

John's life took such a different turn when he met Nancy and then came to know her parents. Today the wonderful legacy of Nancy's parents is reaching beyond their own family to their grandchildren.

But there is more to John's story. Because of the problems in his childhood home, the relationships among him and his sister and brother, Martha and Bob, had always been strained. The three tended to avoid each other because contact between them brought back the terrible feelings from childhood. As John learned more of the values of a close and loving family, he tried to have more contact with Martha and Bob. At first this was painful, especially for Martha and Bob, who were both in troubled marriages. John continued to keep in touch with them, and eventually they all spent a Christmas together.

"We talked about how terrible our Christmas holidays were as children. We talked and we cried. It was painful, but it was good. It was the first time we had ever talked about our pain with each other."

John is looking forward to the time when the three of them can experience real warmth and love for each other. He believes it will happen. His only regret is that no healing can take place with their parents, who died several years ago.

John's story demonstrates how a family that experiences high self-esteem pulls together. John received such affirming response from Nancy's parents that he was able to reach out to his two siblings, wanting to come together even though for years they had been apart. A family with high self-esteem enjoys being together and also keeping in touch when they are apart. The good feelings they have about each other provide a wonderful sense of stability and security in a pressured world. These positive feelings are determined primarily by the legacy of older family members, including those who have died.

LEGACIES FOR OUR CHILDREN'S CHARACTER

All the legacies we leave our children will affect their personal character. Three nonmaterial legacies greatly influence our children, so let's consider each: the moral, spiritual, and emotional legacies.

A Moral Legacy

Morality has to do with our belief of what is right and wrong. The moral legacy we leave our children—how well they internalize our standards of right and wrong—usually reflects how well we modeled our own moral code. We may never have put that code into writing, but we carry it around every day.

Our children discover our moral code by listening to us. When we say, "Don't ever steal," we are revealing that we believe stealing is wrong. When a father says, "Always help others when you can," he is stating his belief that it is right to help others when it is in one's power to do so. Parents make such statements throughout their lifetime, and children hear and mentally record them. They observe our lives and see how closely we live by our professed morality. The closer our behavior corresponds to our stated beliefs about right and wrong, the more respect our children have for us and the greater our moral legacy.

Beth acknowledged the moral legacy she had received when she said at her mother's funeral, "I know that my mother is not perfect, but she came as close as anyone I've ever known. She taught us what was right and wrong and, more importantly, she modeled it for us. On the occasions when she did wrong, she always admitted it and asked our forgiveness.

"I remember the one and only time she ever slapped me. I had begged her all afternoon to take me to the park. She was mopping the floors and was extremely tired. When I asked her for the umpteenth time, 'Momma, please take me to the park,' she slapped me. Then, immediately she dropped her mop, fell to her knees, and said, 'Oh Darling, I'm so sorry. I should not have slapped you. Please forgive me.' She gave me a long hug until I stopped crying.

"We kissed each other and she said, 'I'll take you to the park as soon as I finish mopping this floor.' I only hope that I can be as good a mother to my two children as she was to me."

On the other hand, Ryan wept as he shared the negative moral legacy he had received from his mother. "I hate to say it, but my mother was all talk. She told us what was right and wrong, but she didn't live by her own teachings. She yelled and screamed at us, and often beat us even when we had done no wrong. If we irritated her in the least way, we could expect that she would lash out either physically or verbally. After my sister and I left home, she started running around on my dad. Eventually she left him and moved in with another man. For the next several years, it was from one man to another. She had always told us that adultery was wrong and that we should never live with someone unless we were married. My sister and I could not believe her behavior. She was doing everything she told us not to do. This went on until she got cancer and died six months later.

Dad took care of her hospital bills and we all went to see her regularly.

"Toward the end, she told us that she was sorry for what she had done. I guess we all forgave her. I know I tried, but it didn't take away the pain. I still have an empty, disappointed feeling when I think about her. I don't suppose it will ever go away."

Beth's and Ryan's responses to their mothers' lives should make clear a guiding principle for improving the moral legacy we're preparing for our children: practice your moral standards. When your children observe a positive pattern, they will often copy it.

As with all legacies, a moral legacy becomes the property of your children when you die. It is theirs to enjoy or endure. From this legacy, they receive encouragement or disappointment. Negative or positive, your children have no choice but to receive your legacy. What they do with it, of course, is their responsibility. Those children who have been given a positive moral legacy receive a valuable asset for future living. Conversely, those who are given a negative moral legacy receive a liability with which they must learn to cope.

A Spiritual Legacy

As morality has to do with what we believe to be right and wrong, so spirituality has to do with what we believe about the nonmaterial world. Even if you don't go to church or the synagogue, your spirituality is pervasive—it's part of who you are. It affects your moral and emotional responses, as well as your financial response. And it will influence your children.

Several years ago, I, Gary, participated in an anthropology field trip to the Caribbean island of Dominica with a group of twelve people. We were there to examine various aspects of the island's culture, and my assignment was to study the spiritual belief system.

In one village I talked with an eighty-two-year-old man who had been one of the early converts of Methodist missionaries. I wanted to talk to him because I heard that he practiced white magic. As Mr. Jim and I walked on the beach, I asked him, "I understand that you do white magic. Is that correct?"

"Now and then."

"Do you see any conflict between white magic and your Methodist religion?" I asked.

"What's wrong with burning a few candles and helping people? I don't do black magic. All of my magic is good."

When I asked for an illustration of how he helped people, he told me this story. "A mother came to me and said that her son had moved to another island to get a job and make money, but that he had been gone many months and had sent her no money. I asked her to bring me a piece of the boy's clothing. She brought an old shirt that he had left behind," Mr. Jim said. "I held the shirt and burned a candle, praying that the boy would remember his mother. In two weeks, she got a letter with a check. That is how I help people." He blended his pagan belief system with his Christian belief system and saw no contradiction between the two.

Why this strange mix of the pagan and the religious? I later discovered that his father had practiced white magic and had taught his son to do so. Many years later, in spite of his conversion to Christianity, Mr. Jim is still influenced by his father's spiritual legacy.

Spiritual belief systems are often very intricate. Major world religions, such as Buddhism, Hinduism, Islam, Judaism, and Christianity, are accompanied by voluminous literature developed through the centuries. But spiritual belief systems may also be very simple and individualistic. The person who says "I believe there is a heaven and that eventually everyone will go there" is expressing his own beliefs in what exists beyond the material world. With the decline of scientific idealism and the rise of individualism and relational isolation, Western culture has spawned a plethora of spiritual belief systems.

Parents can be certain that their children will encounter some of these belief systems. Whether or not they embrace those beliefs has a lot to do with the parents' spiritual legacy. All of us are in the process of leaving a spiritual legacy, whether we realize it or not. The spiritual legacy we leave our children depends on how closely our behavior correlates with our expressed beliefs. The more positive the correlation, the more respect our children will have for us and the more positive our spiritual legacy will be.

Rick has received a strong religious legacy from his mother. When he was twenty-three his mother died, but Rick was confident. "One thing I know for sure," he said. "My mother is in heaven. My mother was a godly woman. When I was little, she read Bible stories to me every night and explained what it meant to be a Christian. She told me about the teachings of Jesus, about His death and resurrection, about God's love and forgiveness. But more importantly, she lived her Christian faith. I saw her practice her beliefs every day. Even in her sickness, her faith was strong. . . . I know I will see her again in heaven."

In contrast, the spiritual legacy Spencer received was anything but positive. He has little interest in spiritual matters, mainly because of an inconsistent father. "My father said he was a Christian, but I never saw any evidence of it. I never saw him read the Bible and seldom heard him pray. He didn't go to church. He often cursed and when he lost his temper, he was anything but a Christian. My poor mother put up with more junk from him than any woman should have to endure. If my father was a Christian, then I don't want to be one."

In many families, the adult children have different value systems than the parents, and some of these parents feel that they have failed and give up hope. Yet, nothing is gained if they become downhearted. Parents need to be beacons of hope, not only for children who have different values, but for the rest of the family. Christian parents who lose heart have forgotten that God is always with us, in good times and bad. He is always ready to help in every situation.

Some parents have also forgotten that an adult child can change. Even when children have drifted away from the faith in which they were raised, loving parents will never give up, but will pray continually. Most important of all, caring parents will remember that their strongest influence on their children is their own example. By demonstrating faithfulness to God, parents are role models of lives well lived. The parents' consistent loyalty to God can be a powerful means of helping adult children return to the flock of the faithful.

To those readers who are Christians, remember that adult children who wander from the Christian faith often return when they have children of their own and realize that these little ones must develop a value system. As new parents, they conclude that the only value system worth having is one based on a deep religious faith and a trust in Jesus Christ. They return to a Christian value system based on grace and forgiveness. Though the adult children may have lost much during their spiritual wandering, becoming parents helps them to realize what they almost fully lost.

It is critical for parents of adult children to hold on to their spiritual heritage, not only for themselves but also to give this legacy to their children and grandchildren. The spiritual needs of our children are great; and passing on a spiritual legacy gives them significance, purpose, and noble values that can benefit future generations.

An Emotional Legacy

The emotional legacy we leave depends largely on how we meet the emotional needs of our children. If those needs are met, they receive love, wholeness, and balance—a positive emotional legacy. But, if they are not met, the children receive insecurity, low self-esteem, and often fear—a negative emotional legacy.

The most fundamental emotional need of children is the need to feel loved. Most parents sincerely love their children, but this does not guarantee that the children will *feel* loved. In chapter 9 we emphasized that each child feels he is loved when parents speak his specific love language and when they love him without conditions, showing a "no matter what" kind of love. When your child's need for unconditional love is met, he will do better in school, have a more positive attitude, need less corrective discipline for misbehavior, and have a more stable emotional life.

Other significant emotional needs are the needs for security or safety, the need for self-worth or significance, the need to belong or be accepted, and the need for productivity or accomplishment. When these are met, children grow up to have a healthy emotional life and are able to cope with the stresses of adult life.

When these needs are not met, however, children grow up with many internal struggles that follow them for decades. As an adult, Barbara lived with such struggles; she never was sure her mother loved her.

"I've finally come to understand that my mother meant well," she said during one counseling session. "It took me a long time to realize this, but it has helped me cope with all the pain. I felt that Mom had no time for me. Her harsh, cutting words rang in my mind for years and her uncontrollable physical abuse left deep emotional scars. When she would punish me, she wouldn't speak to me or look at me for several days. When I'd ask if she loved me, she would reply, 'It doesn't do any good to discipline a kid and then turn around and love up on them.'

"I never heard my mother say she loved me. The only time she would touch me was when I was sick. I'd do anything to try to please her.

"I know now that Mom's alcoholism had a lot to do with the way she treated me, but at the time, I didn't understand that. I just felt she didn't love me. I always struggled with self-esteem and felt that I could never accomplish anything. No matter what I did, it was never good enough. I know now that this is not true, but it took a lot of counseling to find healing from the wounds of my childhood. I tried to help Mom when she was sick, and I hope she knew that I loved her. But even in her sickness, I could never really feel close to her. When she died, I went into a deep depression, because I knew that things could never be any different. I have found a measure of healing, but I still feel a great disappointment that I never felt close to my mother." Thousands of other adult children can identify with the kind of pain Barbara has experienced.

THE FINANCIAL LEGACY

It should be clear that the financial legacy we leave our children is far less important than the moral, spiritual, and emotional legacies. However, most parents collect a lot of "stuff" throughout their lifetime—a house, cars, furniture, clothes, books, jewelry, and money. This material stuff is a tangible way to say "I love you"; all of it will be left to others at the time of our death. And it will communicate to our children our care—or lack of it—for their welfare. The way it is left often connects with the other legacies we have talked about, as does the response of children to what they receive.

Most parents want to pass their wealth along to their children and others. An ancient Hebrew proverb says, "A good man leaves an inheritance for his children's children, but a sinner's wealth is stored up for the righteous."[1] The idea was that a sinner, one who lives for himself, will end up having his wealth distributed to others involuntarily—even to those he does not like—while "a good man," one who lives with others in mind, will consciously leave an inheritance for future generations. The question for us is how "good" parents will distribute this inheritance so that it will be a blessing and not a curse to our descendants.

Most of us have seen the devastation of young adults who have received enormous financial inheritances that they were unprepared to handle. Such financial legacies can remove a young person's motivation for productivity and lessen her potential contribution to society. German poet Johann Wolfgang von Goethe wrote, "What from your father's heritage is lent, earn it anew to really possess it."[2] Unfortunately, many young adults who receive large financial sums fail to "really possess it." They hold it in small regard, or use it as they please.

So, how do parents responsibly leave a financial inheritance to their children and their grandchildren? If the inheritance is relatively small, the task is simple, although it is still important to have a will and designate who is to receive what. When the value of an estate increases, the process of dispensing the legacy becomes more complicated. In the affluence of Western culture, many parents accumulate thousands or even millions in assets. Passing this legacy on in a responsible manner is a concern for many, and this section considers several ideas that may be helpful. First, let's meet the Samuels, who themselves were concerned about this legacy.

The Samuels' Strategy

Ben and Joyce Samuel had been married for forty-four years and had three married children and grandchildren. They lived in the large house where they had raised their children. Some years after retirement, they decided to scale down, get a smaller house, and dispose of some furnishings.

They discussed their decision with the children and asked if any of them wanted to buy the house. Since none of them did, they sold the house and found a new one they liked. Then they selected the furnishings they wanted to give away and had an appraiser put a value on them.

Then Ben and Joyce invited the three children to the house to choose what they wanted. The guidelines were three: At the end of the process, each child would have a similar dollar amount; if one was over, he would pay the difference to the other two. All the children had to agree on each choice. If two or more of them wanted the same object, they would auction it off to the highest bidder, thus raising the value of that piece. When the selections were all made, Ben and Joyce were pleased that none of their children had disagreed with the choices of the others and that everyone was happy with what they had received.

Such a plan helped to avoid resentment and misunderstanding among the children. Proper, thoughtful financial arrangements will be fair, equitable, and thoughtful, modeling positive negotiation and maintaining positive relationships among family members.

Once Ben and Joyce had moved to their new home, they began to assess their monetary estate and realized that they had almost two million dollars in stocks, bonds, and CDs. Since their children were raising their families and needed the money more now than they would later, they checked with their accountant and found that the tax laws allowed each of them to give up to $13,000 per year to their child and an additional $10,000 to the child's spouse as nontaxable income. Thus Ben and Joyce could give over $40,000 to each couple per year.

The Samuels decided that for the next five years, they would give each of the three couples $20,000, thus reducing their assets by $300,000. They explained to their children that this would reduce their inheritance, and also suggested that the children might want to think of setting the money aside for the grandchildren's college education, although the Samuels added that they were free to do what they wanted with the money. In dispensing of some of their assets, Ben and Joyce brought their total worth below $1 million, thus assuring themselves that there would be no federal inheritance tax on their estate if they died in the next five years.

At the end of the five years, their stock assets had increased and so they decided to establish a $500,000 trust fund whose capital gains and dividends would go toward their grandchildren's college education. They developed a formula giving each grandchild an equal amount for the four undergraduate years. Whatever funds remained at the end would be held in perpetuity for the great-grandchildren's education.

At the same time, Ben and Joyce revised their wills and told their children what they had done. Each will left the total assets to the spouse; after both were gone, the proceeds would be distributed in the following way: 10 percent to the church they had attended for thirty years; 10 percent each to their college alma maters; 10 percent to their favorite charity; and the remaining 60 percent to be divided equally among the three children. Their household and personal belongings were also to be distributed among the children in the same manner that the earlier items had been. The house was to be sold and the proceeds become part of the estate.

By telling their children their plans, they avoided misunderstandings and future "surprises." They also conveyed what was important to them and revealed their priorities. The children came first and were equal, 20 percent each — but charities, education, and church also were important, each receiving 10 percent.

When Ben died at age seventy-nine, the estate went to Joyce. Four years later, declining health convinced her that she would be better off in an assisted-living facility. She asked the children to help her find such a place and also to help her sell the house and distribute all the items she would not need in her new setting.

Joyce was continuing in the tradition she and Ben had established of seeking to be responsible stewards of their financial legacy. When she died six years later, the settlement of her estate went smoothly in keeping with her will. The children were deeply appreciative of what their parents had done for them through the years, and they received their inheritance with grateful hearts, hoping that they could be as responsible in managing their own financial assets.

Four Guidelines for a Strong Financial Legacy

The Samuels demonstrated several important aspects of passing on a financial legacy. As mentioned, they made fair and equitable arrangements, and in their percentages they revealed their priorities to their children. And in four areas of handling their estate, they showed good stewardship:

1. They knew that some of the money could be given to children before the death of the parents. Giving your offspring part of the estate early is often a wise tax move and proves helpful to the family.

2. They knew the value of consulting an accountant as they made their decisions. Accountants are usually aware of changing tax laws and often can save clients thousands of dollars by their suggestions.

3. They demonstrated that parents can help their children through various financial vehicles.

4. Their actions underlined the importance of a will. To leave any size estate without a will is to allow the state to dictate how the estate will be distributed.

Many families have particular situations for which they need to seek expert help. For instance, when parents have a child who is physically impaired and needs special care, a child who is mentally or emotionally unable to handle money, or a child following a destructive lifestyle, they need to make financial plans that will provide the care that is needed but within wise guidelines.

A LEGACY OF MEMORIES

Positive Memories Will Sustain

As parents of adult children, we will also leave a legacy of memories. In one sense, memories are all any of us possess of the past, and we should be doing our best to ensure that our children have positive memories that can sustain them in the years to come.

However, the memories of shared activities are not as vital as the feelings we had and have about those events. Our most important feelings are the ones we have in everyday life, for they exert a powerful influence on our long-term memory. Because of this, the way we parents conduct ourselves over the long haul is what really counts. It is crucial that we take care to treat family members with courtesy, respect, kindness, love, and gentleness. Also, we should avoid anger, criticism, harshness, and loudness as much as possible. Yes, we will all make mistakes, but if we are honest with ourselves, we can identify those mistakes and seek to avoid repeating the behaviors.

Personal Character Has Great Impact

We have talked about various legacies we leave those who follow us. The most important legacy we can leave is our personal character and integrity. This legacy has the greatest impact on how we are remembered, by our children and in generations to follow. The obituaries of yesteryear told of the character of the person who had died. And though today's death notices seldom tell whether the individual was kind or humble or generous, the qualities of character are just as important now as they were when our grandparents were young. No matter how a person tries to hide what he is, the truth always becomes known.

There is nothing that hurts as much as a negative change in a parent's integrity and behavior. When a person rejects the values she has instilled in her children, it is a blow that will stun children to a degree from which they may never recover. The most common example today is a person who has been a good parent and spouse and then decides that he needs a change and divorces his spouse. This is so prevalent today that many people believe it is normal. Another growing phenomenon is older adults choosing to live together though unmarried.

Carol, a sixty-eight-year-old widow, brought great pain to her daughter when she decided to live with a sixty-six-year-old widower. "I'm not sure I love him," she said, "but I enjoy being with him, and it will save both of us a lot of money. If the young people can do it, why can't we?"

"Because you are my mother," her forty-five-year-old daughter said. "What kind of example do you think this sets for Jennifer and Traci? I can't believe you're doing this. Don't you have any concern for your own grandchildren?"

Carol's behavior contradicted what she had taught her daughter as a young adult. In fact, Carol had often criticized younger couples who lived together without being married. Carol's legacy is in jeopardy. When Jennifer and Traci heard about their grandmother's behavior, they were very upset and confused. She is in danger of losing the respect of those she loves most.

It is not easy to maintain your character and integrity over many years. This is especially true when sacrifice is called for, and all of us meet situations where it is. Thank God for those who are able to take care of their responsibilities over a lifetime and who are willing to give up what they desire for the sake of those in their care. Giving oneself for the sake of others is increasingly rare.

Our society places little value on sacrificial living, on maintaining one's principles, on telling the truth, or on keeping promises. In such an environment, it takes real strength of character and all the support we can find to live righteously. Yet, though society may not praise people of sound character, their children and grandchildren dearly love and appreciate them.

Character Is . . .

We talk of character and integrity, and yet perhaps we need to define them. We want our children to have these qualities, but just what does this mean? Character is the totality of who we genuinely are inside. It is all that we think and feel, what we truthfully stand for, which is expressed in our pattern of behavior.

Integrity is a part of our character and is best known by three behaviors:

- Telling the truth
- Keeping one's promises
- Taking responsibility for one's behavior

All of us have fallen short at times, but we should not give up. If we need to make restitution, we can do so. We can ask forgiveness and make necessary amends.

A by-product of good character is a legacy of stability, when a parent has made good decisions and exhibited clear thinking over many years. Children watch when parents go through tough times and they learn how to handle difficult situations from what they see. Where the parents have given this legacy of stability, the adult children will ask in their own troubled times, "What would Mom and Dad do? How would they think this through? What advice would they seek from others? How long would they allow themselves to decide what to do? How would they pray about it? How would they know when the decision had to be made?"

THE POWER OF PRAYER

We should mention one other powerful vehicle for influencing adult children: prayer. In recent years, social researchers have begun to take seriously the influence of prayer. Numerous studies have shown that the healing process in persons treated by physicians is more effective if the treatment is accompanied by prayer.[3] These researchers are discovering what sincere religious people have always known—prayer changes things and people.

For those in the Judeo-Christian tradition, prayer assumes the existence of a personal and infinite God who cares deeply about His creatures and who has invited them to reciprocate His love. Jews know the love of being called God's chosen people;[4] Christians believe that love is demonstrated by God sending His Son, Jesus of Nazareth, as a sacrifice for people's transgressions.[5] It is this reciprocating love relationship that many have found to be the most satisfying of all relationships and that profoundly affects family dynamics.

The heart of your legacy to your children is not financial but spiritual. Praying for your children daily is a living legacy that can influence their behavior now and for years to come. The praying parent not only becomes a wiser person but is forever an influential parent.

In his will, American patriot Patrick Henry yearned to add to his legacy a spiritual dimension based on his religious faith:

> I have now disposed of all my property to my family. There is one thing more I wish I could give them, and that is faith in Jesus Christ. If they had that and I had not given them one shilling, they would be rich; and if I had not given them that, and had given them all the world, they would be poor indeed.[6]

As you give these legacies—moral, spiritual, emotional, and financial—be grateful that you have the opportunity of watching your children enter adulthood and continue the legacy you have begun. Remember that they are on their own, yet you can continue to influence them for good. Through your character and integrity, you may influence them to adopt your pattern. Through your prayer, you can find both peace for yourself and influence upon your children's spiritual lives. Parenting your adult child at times may be challenging, even difficult, but it is a blessing too, as you influence the next generation and generations to come.

notes

Chapter 1: Getting to Know Today's Adult Child

1. Jeffrey Arnett, *Emerging Adulthood: The Winding Road from the Late Teens through the Twenties* (New York: Oxford University Press USA, 2006) 3–4.
2. As quoted in Marcia Mogelonsky, *American Demographics*, May 1996, 30.
3. "Millennials: A Portrait of Generation Next," Pew Research Forum, 2010 (pewsocialtrends.org).

Chapter 2: When Your Adult Child Is Not Succeeding

1. God often is described as a father, and the Scriptures indicate He has the compassionate heart of a father. See Psalm 103:13–15; Luke 15:20–24; 2 Corinthians 1:3–4.
2. For example, see Acts 7:37–42.
3. See 2 Thessalonians 3:10.
4. Proverbs 18:21.

Chapter 3: When the Nest Isn't Emptying

1. Valerie Wiener, *The Nesting Syndrome* (Minneapolis: Fairview, 1997), 45.
2. Ibid., 47.
3. Judith Martin (Miss Manners), "Adult Children and Parents Can Live Happily Together," *The South Bend Tribune*, 22 March 1998.
4. Ibid.

Chapter 5: Major Hurdles to Independence

1. Laura A. Pratt, PhD, and Debra J. Brody, MPH, "Depression in the United States Household Population, 2005–2006," NCHS Data Brief-No 7-Sept 08, cdc.gov.
2. Edwin L. Klingelhofer, *Coping with Your Grown Children* (Clifton, N.J.: The Humana Press, 1989), 187.
3. "Effects of Alcoholism on Families," learn-about-Alcoholism.com.
4. Amar N. Bhandary et al., "Pharmacology in Adults with ADHD," *Psychiatric Annals* 27, no. 8 (August 1997): 545.
5. Paul Wender, "Attention Deficit Disorder in Adults," *Psychiatric Annals* 27, no. 8 (August 1997): 561.

Chapter 6: Conflicts over Lifestyle Issues

1. Such a discovery is especially difficult for Christian and Jewish parents who believe the Scriptures' injunctions against homosexuality.
2. 1 Corinthians 6:9, 11.
3. Though three studies in the early 1990s "seemed to suggest that homosexuality's roots were genetic," a *Newsweek* report concluded: "The studies were small and the conclusions cautious. . . . The data has never been replicated." John Leland and Mark Miller, "Can Gays 'Convert'?" *Newsweek*, 17 August 1998, 47.
4. Romans 3:23.
5. John 8:7.
6. See 1 Peter 2:24; Romans 8:1.
7. Del DeHart, "Letters to the Editor," *Today's Christian Doctor*, Summer 1997, 4.
8. For a compilation of research, see Glenn T. Stanton, *Why Marriage Matters* (Colorado Springs: Pinion, 1997).
9. The Bible calls upon men and women who need wisdom to pray for it, and promises peace when we do pray. See, for example, James 1:5 and Philippians 4:6–7.

Chapter 7: Becoming an In-Law and a Grandparent

1. Arthur Kornhaber and Kenneth Woodward, *Grandparents/Grandchildren: The Vital Connection* (New Brunswick, N.J.: Transaction, 1991).
2. Proverbs 17:6.
3. Research from aarp.org/relationships/grandparenting.

Chapter 8: Meeting Your Own Needs

1. Matthew 20:28.
2. These are steps two and three of the Twelve Steps of Alcoholics Anonymous. *Alcoholics Anonymous* (New York: Alcoholics Anonymous World Services, Inc., 1979), 59.
3. God's justice, care, and understanding are emphasized in several Scriptures, including Exodus 34:6; Psalm 75:2; 1 Peter 2:24; 5:7.
4. Matthew 6:12. In Ephesians 4:32, Christians are told to forgive "each other, just as in Christ God forgave you."

5. The apostle John wrote that if we confess to God our sins, He "will forgive us our sins and purify us from all unrighteousness" (1 John 1:9). It is at this point that the parent is then able to accept forgiveness from God and from the adult child.
6. Shauna L. Smith, *Making Peace with Your Adult Children* (New York: Plenum Press, 1991), 241.
7. Barbara Smalley, "How to Think the Stress Away!" *Woman's World*, 23 June 1998, 27.
8. Ibid.
9. Ibid.

Chapter 9: Building a Confident, Growing Relationship

1. Michael V. Bloom, "Leaving Home: A Family Transition," in Jonathan Bloom-Feshbach and Sally Bloom-Feshbach, *The Psychology of Separation and Loss: Perspective on Development, Life Transition and Clinical Practice* (San Francisco: Jossey-Bass, 1987). The five stages are outlined in Larry V. Stockman, *Grown-Up Children Who Won't Grow Up* (Rocklin, Calif.: Prima, 1990), 55.
2. The full proverb, "Train a child in the way he should go, and when he is old he will not turn from it" (Proverbs 22:6), was written by Solomon.
3. Psalm 127:3; 103:17, *New American Standard Bible*.

Chapter 10: Leaving Your Child a Positive Legacy

1. Proverbs 13:22.
2. Quoted in George W. Sweeting, *Who Said That?* (Chicago: Moody, 1995), 232.
3. For instance, a 1988 study showed patients who were prayed for had fewer complications during recovery; and a 1998 study indicated those who attended a religious service and prayed or studied the Bible once a day were 40 percent less likely to have high blood pressure than the general public; see Robert Davis, "Prayer Can Lower Blood Presssure," *USA Today*, 11 August 1998, 1D. For a summary of various research projects, see Malcom McConnell, "Faith Can Help You Heal," *Reader's Digest*, October 1998, 109–113.
4. Known as the children of Israel in the Bible, Jews are called both the "chosen" people (see Deuteronomy 7:6–8) and "the apple of His eye" (Deuteronomy 32:9–10), an expression of closeness and care.
5. See Romans 5:8 and 1 John 4:19.
6. Billy Graham, *Facing Death and the Life After* (Minneapolis: Grason, 1987), 31.

Learning your love language—and that of your spouse, teen, and child—might be the easiest and most important thing you ever learn. The assessments featured at www.5lovelanguages.com make it easy to discover your love language. Simply take one of our short profiles and find out how you and your loved one express and interpret love.

Right away, you can make a concerted effort to speak his or her primary language. It might not come naturally, but even the effort will be appreciated.

This dynamic new site is also full of other helpful features—links to other resources, free stuff, upcoming events, podcasts, video, and more—all designed to encourage you and strengthen your relationships. We want to help you feel loved, and effectively communicate love to others.

VISIT 5LOVELANGUAGES.COM

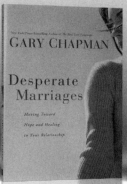
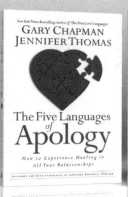
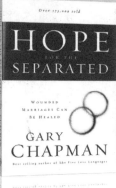

ANGER

Many of us need help with anger. But can anger be used for good? Yes, says Dr. Gary Chapman, who shows us how we can move anger "from one side to another"—toward love.

DESPERATE MARRIAGES

Are you living in a seriously flawed marriage? Gary Chapman offers hope. Discover practical and permanent solutions and take positive steps to change your marriage.

THE FIVE LANGUAGES OF APOLOGY

How many ways are there to say "I'm sorry?" Well, it depends on your language of apology. Just as you have a different love language, you also hear and express the words and gestures of apology in a different language. Bestselling author Gary Chapman teams with counselor Jennifer Thomas to explore the different languages of apology.

HOPE FOR THE SEPARATED

You knew that separation and divorce are common in marriage—but you never thought it would happen to you. Whether you're looking for a way to make your marriage work or just looking for a way out, what you really need is hope.